MY MEDITERRANEAN COOKBOOK 2022

DELICIOUS RECIPES EASY TO MAKE

TO SURPRISE YOUR FAMILY

JENNA LOPEZ

Table of Contents

Sea Bass in a Pocket 9
Creamy Smoked Salmon Pasta 11
Slow Cooker Greek Chicken 13
Chicken Gyros 15
Slow Cooker Chicken Cassoulet 17
Greek Style Turkey Roast 20
Garlic Chicken with Couscous 22
Chicken Karahi 24
Chicken Cacciatore with Orzo 26
Slow Cooked Daube Provencal 28
Osso Bucco 30
Slow Cooker Beef Bourguignon 32
Balsamic Beef 35
Veal Pot Roast 37
Mediterranean Rice and Sausage 39
Spanish Meatballs 40
Cauliflower Steaks with Olive Citrus Sauce 42
Pistachio Mint Pesto Pasta 44
Burst Cherry Tomato Sauce with Angel Hair Pasta 46
Baked Tofu with Sun-Dried Tomatoes and Artichokes 48
Baked Mediterranean Tempeh with Tomatoes and Garlic 50
Roasted Portobello Mushrooms with Kale and Red Onion 53
Ricotta, Basil, and Pistachio–Stuffed Zucchini 57
Farro with Roasted Tomatoes and Mushrooms 59

Baked Orzo with Eggplant, Swiss Chard, and Mozzarella	62
Barley Risotto with Tomatoes	64
Chickpeas and Kale with Spicy Pomodoro Sauce	66
Roasted Feta with Kale and Lemon Yogurt	68
Roasted Eggplant and Chickpeas with Tomato Sauce	70
Baked Falafel Sliders	72
Portobello Caprese	74
Mushroom and Cheese Stuffed Tomatoes	76
Tabbouleh	78
Spicy Broccoli Rabe And Artichoke Hearts	80
Shakshuka	82
Spanakopita	84
Tagine	86
Citrus Pistachios and Asparagus	88
Tomato and Parsley Stuffed Eggplant	90
Ratatouille	92
Gemista	94
Stuffed Cabbage Rolls	96
Brussels Sprouts with Balsamic Glaze	98
Spinach Salad with Citrus Vinaigrette	100
Simple Celery and Orange Salad	101
Fried Eggplant Rolls	103
Roasted Veggies and Brown Rice Bowl	105
Cauliflower Hash with Carrots	107
Garlicky Zucchini Cubes with Mint	108
Zucchini and Artichokes Bowl with Faro	109
5-Ingredient Zucchini Fritters	111

Moroccan Tagine with Vegetables	113
Chickpea Lettuce Wraps with Celery	115
Grilled Vegetable Skewers	116
Stuffed Portobello Mushroom with Tomatoes	118
Wilted Dandelion Greens with Sweet Onion	120
Celery and Mustard Greens	121
Vegetable and Tofu Scramble	122
Simple Zoodles	124
Lentil and Tomato Collard Wraps	125
Mediterranean Veggie Bowl	127
Grilled Veggie and Hummus Wrap	129
Spanish Green Beans	131
Rustic Cauliflower and Carrot Hash	132
Roasted Cauliflower and Tomatoes	133
Roasted Acorn Squash	135
Sautéed Garlic Spinach	137
Garlicky Sautéed Zucchini with Mint	138
Stewed Okra	139
Sweet Veggie-Stuffed Peppers	140
Moussaka Eggplant	142
Vegetable-Stuffed Grape Leaves	144
Grilled Eggplant Rolls	146
Crispy Zucchini Fritters	148
Cheesy Spinach Pies	150
Cucumber Sandwich Bites	152
Yogurt Dip	153
Tomato Bruschetta	154

Olives and Cheese Stuffed Tomatoes	156
Pepper Tapenade	157
Coriander Falafel	158
Red Pepper Hummus	160
White Bean Dip	161
Hummus with Ground Lamb	162
Eggplant Dip	163
Veggie Fritters	164
Bulgur Lamb Meatballs	166
Cucumber Bites	168
Stuffed Avocado	169
Wrapped Plums	170
Marinated Feta and Artichokes	171
Tuna Croquettes	172
Smoked Salmon Crudités	174
Citrus-Marinated Olives	175
Olive Tapenade with Anchovies	176
Greek Deviled Eggs	178
Manchego Crackers	180
Burrata Caprese Stack	182
Zucchini-Ricotta Fritters with Lemon-Garlic Aioli	183
Salmon-Stuffed Cucumbers	185
Goat Cheese–Mackerel Pâté	186
Taste of the Mediterranean Fat Bombs	188
Avocado Gazpacho	189
Crab Cake Lettuce Cups	191
Orange-Tarragon Chicken Salad Wrap	193

Feta and Quinoa Stuffed Mushrooms 195
Five-Ingredient Falafel with Garlic-Yogurt Sauce 197
Lemon Shrimp with Garlic Olive Oil 199
Crispy Green Bean Fries with Lemon-Yogurt Sauce 201
Homemade Sea Salt Pita Chips 203
Baked Spanakopita Dip 204
Roasted Pearl Onion Dip 206
Red Pepper Tapenade 208
Greek Potato Skins with Olives and Feta 210
Artichoke and Olive Pita Flatbread 212
Mini Crab Cakes 214
Zucchini Feta Roulades 216

Sea Bass in a Pocket

Preparation Time : 10 minutes

Cooking Time : 25 minutes

Servings : 4

Difficulty Level : Average

Ingredients:

- 4 sea bass fillets
- 4 sliced garlic cloves
- 1 sliced celery stalk
- 1 sliced zucchini
- 1 c. halved cherry tomatoes halved
- 1 shallot, sliced
- 1 tsp. dried oregano
- Salt and pepper

Directions:

Mix the garlic, celery, zucchini, tomatoes, shallot, and oregano in a bowl. Add salt and pepper to taste. Take 4 sheets of baking paper and arrange them on your working surface. Spoon the vegetable mixture in the center of each sheet.

Top with a fish fillet then wrap the paper well so it resembles a pocket. Place the wrapped fish in a baking tray and cook in the preheated oven at 350 F/176 C for 15 minutes. Serve the fish warm and fresh.

Nutrition (for 100g): 149 Calories 2.8g Fat 5.2g Carbohydrates 25.2g Protein 696mg Sodium

Creamy Smoked Salmon Pasta

Preparation Time : 5 minutes

Cooking Time : 35 minutes

Servings : 4

Difficulty Level : Average

Ingredients:

- 2 tbsps. olive oil
- 2 chopped garlic cloves
- 1 shallot, chopped
- 4 oz. or 113 g chopped salmon, smoked
- 1 c. green peas
- 1 c. heavy cream
- Salt and pepper
- 1 pinch chili flakes
- 8 oz. or 230 g penne pasta
- 6 c. water

Directions:

Place skillet on medium-high heat and add oil. Add the garlic and shallot. Cook for 5 minutes or until softened. Add peas, salt, pepper, and chili flakes. Cook for 10 minutes

Add the salmon, and continue cooking for 5-7 minutes more. Add heavy cream, reduce heat and cook for an extra 5 minutes.

In the meantime, place a pan with water and salt to your taste on high heat as soon as it boils, add penne pasta and cook for 8-10 minutes or until softened Drain the pasta, add to the salmon sauce and serve

Nutrition (for 100g): 393 Calories 20.8g Fat 38g Carbohydrates 3g Protein 836mg Sodium

Slow Cooker Greek Chicken

Preparation Time : 20 minutes

Cooking Time : 3 hours

Servings : 4

Difficulty Level : Average

Ingredients:

- 1 tablespoon extra-virgin olive oil
- 2 pounds boneless, chicken breasts
- ½ tsp kosher salt
- ¼ tsp black pepper
- 1 (12-ounce) jar roasted red peppers
- 1 cup Kalamata olives
- 1 medium red onion, cut into chunks
- 3 tablespoons red wine vinegar
- 1 tablespoon minced garlic
- 1 teaspoon honey
- 1 teaspoon dried oregano
- 1 teaspoon dried thyme
- ½ cup feta cheese (optional, for serving)
- Chopped fresh herbs: any mix of basil, parsley, or thyme (optional, for serving)

Directions:

Brush slow cooker with nonstick cooking spray or olive oil. Cook the olive oil in a large skillet. Season both side of the chicken breasts. Once the oil is hot, add the chicken breasts and sear on both sides (about 3 minutes).

Once cooked, transfer it to the slow cooker. Add the red peppers, olives, and red onion to the chicken breasts. Try to place the vegetables around the chicken and not directly on top.

In a small bowl, mix the vinegar, garlic, honey, oregano, and thyme. Once combined, pour it over the chicken. Cook the chicken on low for 3 hours or until no longer pink in the middle. Serve with crumbled feta cheese and fresh herbs.

Nutrition (for 100g): 399 Calories 17g Fat 12g Carbohydrates 50g Protein 793mg Sodium

Chicken Gyros

Preparation Time : 10 minutes

Cooking Time : 4 hours

Servings : 4

Difficulty Level : Average

Ingredients:

- 2 lbs. boneless chicken breasts or chicken tenders
- Juice of one lemon
- 3 cloves garlic
- 2 teaspoons red wine vinegar
- 2–3 tablespoons olive oil
- ½ cup Greek yogurt
- 2 teaspoons dried oregano
- 2–4 teaspoons Greek seasoning
- ½ small red onion, chopped
- 2 tablespoons dill weed
- Tzatziki Sauce
- 1 cup plain Greek yogurt
- 1 tablespoon dill weed
- 1 small English cucumber, chopped
- Pinch of salt and pepper
- 1 teaspoon onion powder
- <u>For Toppings:</u>

- Tomatoes
- Chopped cucumbers
- Chopped red onion
- Diced feta cheese
- Crumbled pita bread

Directions:

Slice the chicken breasts into cubes and place in the slow cooker. Add the lemon juice, garlic, vinegar, olive oil, Greek yogurt, oregano, Greek seasoning, red onion, and dill to the slow cooker and stir to make sure everything is well combined.

Cook on low for 5–6 hours or on high for 2–3 hours. In the meantime, incorporate all ingredients for the tzatziki sauce and stir. When well mixed, put in the refrigerator until the chicken is done.

When the chicken has finished cooking, serve with pita bread and any or all of the toppings listed above.

Nutrition (for 100g): 317 Calories 7.4g Fat 36.1g Carbohydrates 28.6g Protein 476mg Sodium

Slow Cooker Chicken Cassoulet

Preparation Time : 10 minutes

Cooking Time : 20 minutes

Servings : 16

Difficulty Level : Average

Ingredients:

- 1 cup dry navy beans, soaked
- 8 bone-in skinless chicken thighs
- 1 Polish sausage, cooked and chopped into bite-sized pieces (optional)
- 1¼ cup tomato juice
- 1 (28-ounce) can halved tomatoes
- 1 tbsp Worcestershire sauce
- 1 tsp instant beef or chicken bouillon granules
- ½ tsp dried basil
- ½ teaspoon dried oregano
- ½ teaspoon paprika
- ½ cup chopped celery
- ½ cup chopped carrot
- ½ cup chopped onion

Directions:

Brush the slow cooker with olive oil or nonstick cooking spray. In a mixing bowl, stir together the tomato juice, tomatoes, Worcestershire sauce, beef bouillon, basil, oregano, and paprika. Make sure the ingredients are well combined.

Place the chicken and sausage into the slow cooker and cover with the tomato juice mixture. Top with celery, carrot, and onion. Cook on low for 10–12 hours.

Nutrition (for 100g): 244 Calories 7g Fat 25g Carbohydrates 21g

Slow Cooker Chicken Provencal

Preparation Time : 5 minutes

Cooking Time : 8 hours

Servings : 4

Difficulty Level : Easy

Ingredients:

- 4 (6-ounce) skinless bone-in chicken breast halves
- 2 teaspoons dried basil
- 1 teaspoon dried thyme
- 1/8 teaspoon salt
- 1/8 teaspoon freshly ground black pepper
- 1 yellow pepper, diced
- 1 red pepper, diced
- 1 (15.5-ounce) can cannellini beans
- 1 (14.5-ounce) can petite tomatoes with basil, garlic, and oregano, undrained

Directions:

Brush the slow cooker with nonstick olive oil. Add all the ingredients to the slow cooker and stir to combine. Cook on low for 8 hours.

Nutrition (for 100g): 304 Calories 4.5g Fat 27.3g Carbohydrates 39.4g Protein 639mg Sodium

Greek Style Turkey Roast

Preparation Time : 20 minutes

Cooking Time : 7 hours and 30 minutes

Servings : 8

Difficulty Level : Average

Ingredients:

- 1 (4-pound) boneless turkey breast, trimmed
- ½ cup chicken broth, divided
- 2 tablespoons fresh lemon juice
- 2 cups chopped onion
- ½ cup pitted Kalamata olives
- ½ cup oil-packed sun-dried tomatoes, thinly sliced
- 1 teaspoon Greek seasoning
- ½ teaspoon salt
- ¼ teaspoon fresh ground black pepper
- 3 tablespoons all-purpose flour (or whole wheat)

Directions:

Brush the slow cooker with nonstick cooking spray or olive oil. Add the turkey, ¼ cup of the chicken broth, lemon juice, onion, olives, sun-dried tomatoes, Greek seasoning, salt and pepper to the slow cooker.

Cook on low for 7 hours. Scourge the flour into the remaining ¼ cup of chicken broth, then stir gently into the slow cooker. Cook for an additional 30 minutes.

Nutrition (for 100g): 341 Calories 19g Fat 12g Carbohydrates 36.4g Protein 639mg Sodium

Garlic Chicken with Couscous

Preparation Time : 25 minutes

Cooking Time : 7 hours

Servings : 4

Difficulty Level : Average

Ingredients:

- 1 whole chicken, cut into pieces
- 1 tablespoon extra-virgin olive oil
- 6 cloves garlic, halved
- 1 cup dry white wine
- 1 cup couscous
- ½ teaspoon salt
- ½ teaspoon pepper
- 1 medium onion, thinly sliced
- 2 teaspoons dried thyme
- 1/3 cup whole wheat flour

Directions:

Cook the olive oil in a heavy skillet. When skillet is hot, add the chicken to sear. Make sure the chicken pieces don't touch each other. Cook with the skin side down for about 3 minutes or until browned.

Brush your slow cooker with nonstick cooking spray or olive oil. Put the onion, garlic, and thyme into the slow cooker and sprinkle with salt and pepper. Stir in the chicken on top of the onions.

In a separate bowl, whisk the flour into the wine until there are no lumps, then pour over the chicken. Cook on low for 7 hours or until done. You can cook on high for 3 hours as well. Serve the chicken over the cooked couscous and spoon sauce over the top.

Nutrition (for 100g): 440 Calories 17.5g Fat 14g Carbohydrates 35.8g Protein 674mg Sodium

Chicken Karahi

Preparation Time : 5 minutes

Cooking Time : 5 hours

Servings : 4

Difficulty Level : Easy

Ingredients:

- 2 lbs. chicken breasts or thighs
- ¼ cup olive oil
- 1 small can tomato paste
- 1 tablespoon butter
- 1 large onion, diced
- ½ cup plain Greek yogurt
- ½ cup water
- 2 tablespoons ginger in garlic paste
- 3 tablespoons fenugreek leaves
- 1 teaspoon ground coriander
- 1 medium tomato
- 1 teaspoon red chili
- 2 green chilies
- 1 teaspoon turmeric
- 1 tablespoon garam masala
- 1 teaspoon cumin powder
- 1 teaspoon sea salt
- ¼ teaspoon nutmeg

Directions:

Brush the slow cooker with nonstick cooking spray. In a small bowl, thoroughly mix all of the spices. Mix in the chicken to the slow cooker, followed by the ingredients' rest, including the spice mixture. Stir until everything is well mixed with the spices.

Cook on low for 4–5 hours. Serve with naan or Italian bread.

Nutrition (for 100g): 345 Calories 9.9g Fat 10g Carbohydrates 53.7g Protein 715mg Sodium

Chicken Cacciatore with Orzo

Preparation Time : 20 minutes

Cooking Time : 4 hours

Servings : 6

Difficulty Level : Easy

Ingredients:

- 2 pounds skin-on chicken thighs
- 1 tablespoon olive oil
- 1 cup mushrooms, quartered
- 3 carrots, chopped
- 1 small jar Kalamata olives
- 2 (14-ounce) cans diced tomatoes
- 1 small can tomato paste
- 1 cup red wine
- 5 garlic cloves
- 1 cup orzo

Directions:

In a large skillet, cook the olive oil. When the oil is heated, add the chicken, skin side down, and sear it. Make sure the pieces of chicken don't touch each other.

When the chicken is browned, add to the slow cooker along with all the ingredients except the orzo. Cook the chicken on low for 2 hours, then add the orzo and cook for an additional 2 hours. Serve with a crusty French bread.

Nutrition (for 100g): 424 Calories 16g Fat 10g Carbohydrates 11g Protein 845mg Sodium

Slow Cooked Daube Provencal

Preparation Time : 15 minutes

Cooking Time : 8 hours

Servings : 8

Difficulty Level : Average

Ingredients:

- 1 tablespoon olive oil
- 10 garlic cloves, minced
- 2 pounds boneless chuck roast
- 1½ teaspoons salt, divided
- ½ teaspoon freshly ground black pepper
- 1 cup dry red wine
- 2 cups carrots, chopped
- 1½ cups onion, chopped
- ½ cup beef broth
- 1 (14-ounce) can diced tomatoes
- 1 tablespoon tomato paste
- 1 teaspoon fresh rosemary, chopped
- 1 teaspoon fresh thyme, chopped
- ½ teaspoon orange zest, grated
- ½ teaspoon ground cinnamon
- ¼ teaspoon ground cloves
- 1 bay leaf

Directions:

Preheat a skillet and then add the olive oil. Add the minced garlic and onions and cook until the onions are soft and the garlic begins to brown.

Add the cubed meat, salt, and pepper and cook until the meat has browned. Transfer the meat to the slow cooker. Mix in the beef broth to the skillet and let simmer for about 3 minutes to deglaze the pan, then pour into slow cooker over the meat.

Incorporate the rest of the ingredients to the slow cooker and stir well to combine. Adjust slow cooker to low and cook for 8 hours, or set to high and cook for 4 hours. Serve with a side of egg noodles, rice or some crusty Italian bread.

Nutrition (for 100g): 547 Calories 30.5g Fat 22g Carbohydrates 45.2g Protein 809mg Sodium

Osso Bucco

Preparation Time : 30 minutes

Cooking Time : 8 hours

Servings : 3

Difficulty Level : Average

Ingredients:

- 4 beef shanks or veal shanks
- 1 teaspoon sea salt
- ½ teaspoon ground black pepper
- 3 tablespoons whole wheat flour
- 1–2 tablespoons olive oil
- 2 medium onions, diced
- 2 medium carrots, diced
- 2 celery stalks, diced
- 4 garlic cloves, minced
- 1 (14-ounce) can diced tomatoes
- 2 teaspoons dried thyme leaves
- ½ cup beef or vegetable stock

Directions:

Season the shanks on both sides, then dip in the flour to coat. Heat a large skillet over high heat. Add the olive oil. Once the oil is hot, add the shanks and brown evenly on both sides. When browned, transfer to the slow cooker.

Pour the stock into the skillet and let simmer for 3–5 minutes while stirring to deglaze the pan. Transfer the rest of the ingredients to the slow cooker and pour the stock from the skillet over the top.

Adjust the slow cooker to low and cook for 8 hours. Serve the Osso Bucco over quinoa, brown rice, or even cauliflower rice.

Nutrition (for 100g): 589 Calories 21.3g Fat 15g Carbohydrates 74.7g Protein 893mg Sodium

Slow Cooker Beef Bourguignon

Preparation Time : 5 minutes

Cooking Time : 8 hours

Servings : 8

Difficulty Level : Difficult

Ingredients:

- 1 tablespoon extra-virgin olive oil
- 6 ounces bacon, roughly chopped
- 3 pounds beef brisket, trimmed of fat, cut into 2-inch cubes
- 1 large carrot, sliced
- 1 large white onion, diced
- 6 cloves garlic, minced and divided
- ½ teaspoon coarse salt
- ½ teaspoon freshly ground pepper
- 2 tablespoons whole wheat
- 12 small pearl onions
- 3 cups red wine (Merlot, Pinot Noir, or Chianti)
- 2 cups beef stock
- 2 tablespoons tomato paste
- 1 beef bouillon cube, crushed
- 1 teaspoon fresh thyme, finely chopped
- 2 tablespoons fresh parsley
- 2 bay leaves
- 2 tablespoons butter or 1 tablespoon olive oil

- 1 pound fresh small white or brown mushrooms, quartered

Directions:

Heat up a skillet over medium-high heat, then add the olive oil. When the oil has heated, cook the bacon until it is crisp, then place it in your slow cooker. Save the bacon fat in the skillet.

Pat dry the beef and cook it in the same skillet with the bacon fat until all sides have the same brown coloring. Transfer to the slow cooker.

Mix in the onions and carrots to the slow cooker and season with the salt and pepper. Stir to combine the ingredients and make sure everything is seasoned.

Stir in the red wine into the skillet and simmer for 4–5 minutes to deglaze the pan, then whisk in the flour, stirring until smooth. Continue cooking until the liquid reduces and thickens a bit.

When the liquid has thickened, pour it into the slow cooker and stir to coat everything with the wine mixture. Add the tomato paste, bouillon cube, thyme, parsley, 4 cloves of garlic, and bay leaf. Adjust your slow cooker to high and cook for 6 hours, or set to low and cook for 8 hours.

Soften the butter or heat the olive oil in a skillet over medium heat. When the oil is hot, stir in the remaining 2 cloves of garlic and cook for about 1 minute before adding the mushrooms. Cook the mushrooms until soft, then add to the slow cooker and mix to combine.

Serve with mashed potatoes, rice or noodles.

Nutrition (for 100g): 672 Calories 32g Fat 15g Carbohydrates 56g Protein 693mg Sodium

Balsamic Beef

Preparation Time : 5 minutes

Cooking Time : 8 hours

Servings : 10

Difficulty Level : Average

Ingredients:

- 2 pounds boneless chuck roast
- 1 tablespoon olive oil
- Rub
- 1 teaspoon garlic powder
- ½ teaspoon onion powder
- 1 teaspoon sea salt
- ½ teaspoon freshly ground black pepper
- Sauce
- ½ cup balsamic vinegar
- 2 tablespoons honey
- 1 tablespoon honey mustard
- 1 cup beef broth
- 1 tablespoon tapioca, whole wheat flour, or cornstarch (to thicken sauce when it is done cooking if desired)

Directions:

Incorporate all of the ingredients for the rub.

In a separate bowl, mix the balsamic vinegar, honey, honey mustard, and beef broth. Coat the roast in olive oil, then rub in the spices from the rub mix. Place the roast in the slow cooker and then pour the sauce over the top. Adjust the slow cooker to low and cook for 8 hours.

If you want to thicken the sauce when the roast is done cooking transfer it from the slow cooker to a serving plate. Then fill the liquid into a saucepan and heat to boiling on the stovetop. Mix the flour until smooth and let simmer until the sauce thickens.

Nutrition (for 100g): 306 Calories 19g Fat 13g Carbohydrates 25g Protein 823mg Sodium

Veal Pot Roast

Preparation Time : 20 minutes

Cooking Time : 5 hours

Servings : 8

Difficulty Level : Average

Ingredients:

- 2 tablespoons olive oil
- Salt and pepper
- 3-pound boneless veal roast, tied
- 4 medium carrots, peeled
- 2 parsnips, peeled and halved
- 2 white turnips, peeled and quartered
- 10 garlic cloves, peeled
- 2 sprigs fresh thyme
- 1 orange, scrubbed and zested
- 1 cup chicken or veal stock

Directions:

Heat a large skillet over medium-high heat. Scour veal roast all over with olive oil, then season with salt and pepper. When the skillet is hot, add the veal roast and sear on all sides. This will take about 3 minutes on every side, but this process seals in the juices and makes the meat succulent.

When cooked, place it to the slow cooker. Toss the carrots, parsnips, turnips, and garlic into the skillet. Stir and cook for about 5 minutes—not all the way through, just to get some of the brown bits from the veal and give them a bit of color.

Transfer the vegetables to the slow cooker, placing them all around the meat. Top the roast with the thyme and the zest from the orange. Cut the orange in half and squeeze the juice over the top of the meat. Add the chicken stock, then cook the roast on low for 5 hours.

Nutrition (for 100g): 426 Calories 12.8g Fat 10g Carbohydrates 48.8g Protein 822mg Sodium

Mediterranean Rice and Sausage

Preparation Time : 15 minutes

Cooking Time : 8 hours

Servings : 6

Difficulty Level : Average

Ingredients:

- 1½ pounds Italian sausage, crumbled
- 1 medium onion, chopped
- 2 tablespoons steak sauce
- 2 cups long grain rice, uncooked
- 1 (14-ounce) can diced tomatoes with juice
- ½ cup water
- 1 medium green pepper, diced

Directions:

Spray your slow cooker with olive oil or nonstick cooking spray. Add the sausage, onion, and steak sauce to the slow cooker. Set on low for 8 to 10 hours.

After 8 hours, add the rice, tomatoes, water and green pepper. Stir to combine thoroughly. Cook an additional 20 to 25 minutes.

Nutrition (for 100g): 650 Calories 36g Fat 11g Carbohydrates 22g Protein 633mg Sodium

Spanish Meatballs

Preparation Time : 20 minutes

Cooking Time : 5 hours

Servings : 6

Difficulty Level : Difficult

Ingredients:

- 1-pound ground turkey
- 1-pound ground pork
- 2 eggs
- 1 (20-ounce) can diced tomatoes
- ¾ cup sweet onion, minced, divided
- ¼ cup plus 1 tablespoon breadcrumbs
- 3 tablespoons fresh parsley, chopped
- 1½ teaspoons cumin
- 1½ teaspoons paprika (sweet or hot)

Directions:

Spray the slow cooker with olive oil.

In a mixing bowl, incorporate the ground meat, eggs, about half of the onions, the breadcrumbs, and the spices.

Wash your hands and mix together until everything is well combined. Do not over-mix, though, as this makes for tough meatballs. Shape into meatballs. How big you make them will obviously determine how many total meatballs you get.

In a skillet, cook 2 tablespoons of olive oil over medium heat. Once hot, mix in the meatballs and brown on all sides. Make sure the balls aren't touching each other so they brown evenly. Once done, transfer them to the slow cooker.

Add the rest of the onions and the tomatoes to the skillet and allow them to cook for a few minutes, scraping the brown bits from the meatballs up to add flavor. Transfer the tomatoes over the meatballs in the slow cooker and cook on low for 5 hours.

Nutrition (for 100g): 372 Calories 21.7g Fat 15g Carbohydrates 28.6 Protein 772mg Sodium

Cauliflower Steaks with Olive Citrus Sauce

Preparation Time : 15 minutes

Cooking Time : 30 minutes

Servings : 4

Difficulty Level : Average

Ingredients:

- 1 or 2 large heads cauliflower
- 1/3 cup extra-virgin olive oil
- ¼ teaspoon kosher salt
- 1/8 teaspoon ground black pepper
- Juice of 1 orange
- Zest of 1 orange
- ¼ cup black olives, pitted and chopped
- 1 tablespoon Dijon or grainy mustard
- 1 tablespoon red wine vinegar
- ½ teaspoon ground coriander

Directions:

Preheat the oven to 400°F. Put parchment paper or foil into the baking sheet. Cut off the stem of the cauliflower so it will sit upright. Slice it vertically into four thick slabs. Place the cauliflower on the prepared baking sheet. Dash with the olive oil, salt, and black pepper. Bake for about 30 minutes.

In a medium bowl, stir the orange juice, orange zest, olives, mustard, vinegar, and coriander; mix well. Serve with the sauce.

Nutrition (for 100g): 265 Calories 21g Fat 4g Carbohydrates 5g Protein 693mg Sodium

Pistachio Mint Pesto Pasta

Preparation Time : 10 minutes

Cooking Time : 10 minutes

Servings : 4

Difficulty Level : Average

Ingredients:

- 8 ounces whole-wheat pasta
- 1 cup fresh mint
- ½ cup fresh basil
- 1/3 cup unsalted pistachios, shelled
- 1 garlic clove, peeled
- ½ teaspoon kosher salt
- Juice of ½ lime
- 1/3 cup extra-virgin olive oil

Directions:

Cook the pasta following the package directions. Drain, reserving ½ cup of the pasta water, and set aside. In a food processor, add the mint, basil, pistachios, garlic, salt, and lime juice. Process until the pistachios are coarsely ground. Stir in the olive oil in a slow, steady stream and process until incorporated.

In a large bowl, incorporate the pasta with the pistachio pesto. If a thinner, more saucy consistency is desired, add some of the reserved pasta water and toss well.

Nutrition (for 100g): 420 Calories 3g Fat 2g Carbohydrates 11g Protein 593mg Sodium

Burst Cherry Tomato Sauce with Angel Hair Pasta

Preparation Time : 10 minutes
Cooking Time : 20 minutes
Servings : 4
Difficulty Level : Average

Ingredients:

- 8 ounces angel hair pasta
- 2 tablespoons extra-virgin olive oil
- 3 garlic cloves, minced
- 3 pints cherry tomatoes
- ½ teaspoon kosher salt
- ¼ teaspoon red pepper flakes
- ¾ cup fresh basil, chopped
- 1 tablespoon white balsamic vinegar (optional)
- ¼ cup grated Parmesan cheese (optional)

Directions:

Cook the pasta following the package directions. Drain and set aside.

Cook the olive oil in a skillet or large sauté pan over medium-high heat. Stir in the garlic and sauté for 30 seconds. Mix in the tomatoes, salt, and red pepper flakes and cook, stirring occasionally, until the tomatoes burst, about 15 minutes.

Take out from the heat and stir in the pasta and basil. Toss together well. (For out-of-season tomatoes, add the vinegar, if desired, and mix well.) Serve.

Nutrition (for 100g): 305 Calories 8g Fat 3g Carbohydrates 11g Protein 559mg Sodium

Baked Tofu with Sun-Dried Tomatoes and Artichokes

Preparation Time : 30 minutes
Cooking Time : 30 minutes
Servings : 4
Difficulty Level : Average

Ingredients:

- 1 (16-ounce) package extra-firm tofu, cut into 1-inch cubes
- 2 tablespoons extra-virgin olive oil, divided
- 2 tablespoons lemon juice, divided
- 1 tablespoon low-sodium soy sauce
- 1 onion, diced
- ½ teaspoon kosher salt
- 2 garlic cloves, minced
- 1 (14-ounce) can artichoke hearts, drained
- 8 sun-dried tomato
- ¼ teaspoon freshly ground black pepper
- 1 tablespoon white wine vinegar
- Zest of 1 lemon
- ¼ cup fresh parsley, chopped

Directions:

Prepare the oven to 400°F. Position the foil or parchment paper into the baking sheet. In a bowl, combine the tofu, 1 tablespoon of the olive oil, 1 tablespoon of the lemon juice, and the soy sauce. Set aside and marinate for 15 to 30 minutes. Arrange the tofu in a single layer on the prepared baking sheet and bake for 20 minutes, turning once, until light golden brown.

Cook the remaining 1 tablespoon olive oil in a large skillet or sauté pan over medium heat. Add the onion and salt; sauté until translucent, 5 to 6 minutes. Mix in the garlic and sauté for 30 seconds. Then put the artichoke hearts, sun-dried tomatoes, and black pepper and sauté for 5 minutes. Add the white wine vinegar and the remaining 1 tablespoon lemon juice and deglaze the pan, scraping up any brown bits. Take the pan from the heat and put in the lemon zest and parsley. Gently mix in the baked tofu.

Nutrition (for 100g): 230 Calories 14g Fat 5g Carbohydrates 14g Protein 593mg Sodium

Baked Mediterranean Tempeh with Tomatoes and Garlic

Preparation Time : 25 minutes, plus 4 hours to marinate
Cooking Time : 35 minutes
Servings : 4
Difficulty Level : Difficult

Ingredients:

- <u>For the Tempeh</u>
- 12 ounces tempeh
- ¼ cup white wine
- 2 tablespoons extra-virgin olive oil
- 2 tablespoons lemon juice
- Zest of 1 lemon
- ¼ teaspoon kosher salt
- ¼ teaspoon freshly ground black pepper
- <u>For the Tomatoes and Garlic Sauce</u>
- 1 tablespoon extra-virgin olive oil
- 1 onion, diced
- 3 garlic cloves, minced
- 1 (14.5-ounce) can no-salt-added crushed tomatoes
- 1 beefsteak tomato, diced
- 1 dried bay leaf
- 1 teaspoon white wine vinegar

- 1 teaspoon lemon juice
- 1 teaspoon dried oregano
- 1 teaspoon dried thyme
- ¾ teaspoon kosher salt
- ¼ cup basil, cut into ribbons

Directions:

To Make the Tempeh

Place the tempeh in a medium saucepan. Fill enough water to cover it by 1 to 2 inches. Bring to a boil over medium-high heat, cover, and lower heat to a simmer. Cook for 10 to 15 minutes. Remove the tempeh, pat dry, cool, and cut into 1-inch cubes.

Mix the white wine, olive oil, lemon juice, lemon zest, salt, and black pepper. Add the tempeh, cover the bowl, put in the refrigerator for 4 hours, or overnight. Preheat the oven to 375°F. Place the marinated tempeh and the marinade in a baking dish and cook for 15 minutes.

To Make the Tomatoes and Garlic Sauce

Cook the olive oil in a large skillet over medium heat. Add the onion and sauté until transparent, 3 to 5 minutes. Mix in the garlic and sauté for 30 seconds. Add the crushed tomatoes, beefsteak tomato, bay leaf, vinegar, lemon juice, oregano, thyme, and salt. Mix well. Simmer for 15 minutes.

Add the baked tempeh to the tomato mixture and gently mix together. Garnish with the basil.

SUBSTITUTION TIP: If you're out of tempeh or simply want to speed up the cooking process, you can swap in a 14.5-ounce can of white beans for the tempeh. Rinse the beans and put them to the sauce with the crushed tomatoes. It still makes a great vegan entrée in half the time!

Nutrition (for 100g): 330 Calories 20g Fat 4g Carbohydrates 18g Protein 693mg Sodium

Roasted Portobello Mushrooms with Kale and Red Onion

Preparation Time : 30 minutes

Cooking Time : 30 minutes

Servings : 4

Difficulty Level : Difficult

Ingredients:

- ¼ cup white wine vinegar
- 3 tablespoons extra-virgin olive oil, divided
- ½ teaspoon honey
- ¾ teaspoon kosher salt, divided
- ¼ teaspoon freshly ground black pepper
- 4 large portobello mushrooms, stems removed
- 1 red onion, julienned
- 2 garlic cloves, minced
- 1 (8-ounce) bunch kale, stemmed and chopped small
- ¼ teaspoon red pepper flakes
- ¼ cup grated Parmesan or Romano cheese

Directions:

Situate parchment paper or foil into the baking sheet. In a medium bowl, whisk together the vinegar, 1½ tablespoons of the olive oil, honey, ¼ teaspoon of the salt, and the black pepper. Lay the mushrooms on the baking sheet and pour the marinade over them. Marinate for 15 to 30 minutes.

Meanwhile, preheat the oven to 400°F. Bake the mushrooms for 20 minutes, turning over halfway through. Heat the remaining 1½ tablespoons olive oil in a large skillet or ovenproof sauté pan over medium-high heat. Add the onion and the remaining ½ teaspoon salt and sauté until golden brown, 5 to 6 minutes. Mix in the garlic and sauté for 30 seconds. Mix in the kale and red pepper flakes and sauté until the kale cooks down, about 5 minutes.

Remove the mushrooms from the oven and increase the temperature to broil. Carefully pour the liquid from the baking sheet into the pan with the kale mixture; mix well. Turn the mushrooms over so that the stem side is facing up. Spoon some of the kale mixture on top of each mushroom. Sprinkle 1 tablespoon Parmesan cheese on top of each. Broil until golden brown.

Nutrition (For 100g): 200 Calories 13g Fat 4g Carbohydrates 8g Protein

Balsamic Marinated Tofu with Basil and Oregano

Preparation Time : 40 minutes

Cooking Time : 30 minutes

Servings : 4

Difficulty Level : Average

Ingredients:

- ¼ cup extra-virgin olive oil
- ¼ cup balsamic vinegar
- 2 tablespoons low-sodium soy sauce
- 3 garlic cloves, grated
- 2 teaspoons pure maple syrup
- Zest of 1 lemon
- 1 teaspoon dried basil
- 1 teaspoon dried oregano
- ½ teaspoon dried thyme
- ½ teaspoon dried sage
- ¼ teaspoon kosher salt
- ¼ teaspoon freshly ground black pepper
- ¼ teaspoon red pepper flakes (optional)
- 1 (16-ounce) block extra firm tofu

Directions:

In a bowl or gallon zip-top bag, mix together the olive oil, vinegar, soy sauce, garlic, maple syrup, lemon zest, basil, oregano, thyme, sage, salt, black pepper, and red pepper flakes, if desired. Add the tofu and mix gently. Put in the refrigerator and marinate for 30 minutes, or up to overnight if you desire.

Prepare the oven to 425°F. Place parchment paper or foil into the baking sheet. Arrange the marinated tofu in a single layer on the prepared baking sheet. Bake for 20 to 30 minutes, flip over halfway through, until slightly crispy.

Nutrition (for 100g): 225 Calories 16g Fat 2g Carbohydrates 13g Protein 493mg Sodium

Ricotta, Basil, and Pistachio–Stuffed Zucchini

Preparation Time : 15 minutes
Cooking Time : 25 minutes
Servings : 4
Difficulty Level : Average

Ingredients:

- 2 medium zucchinis, halved lengthwise
- 1 tablespoon extra-virgin olive oil
- 1 onion, diced
- 1 teaspoon kosher salt
- 2 garlic cloves, minced
- ¾ cup ricotta cheese
- ¼ cup unsalted pistachios, shelled and chopped
- ¼ cup fresh basil, chopped
- 1 large egg, beaten
- ¼ teaspoon freshly ground black pepper

Directions:

Ready the oven to 425°F. Situate parchment paper or foil into the baking sheet. Scoop out the seeds/pulp from the zucchini, leaving ¼-inch flesh around the edges. Situate the pulp to a cutting board and chop off the pulp.

Cook the olive oil in a sauté pan over medium heat. Add the onion, pulp, and salt and sauté about 5 minutes. Add the garlic and sauté 30 seconds. Mix the ricotta cheese, pistachios, basil, egg, and black pepper. Add the onion mixture and mix well.

Place the 4 zucchini halves on the prepared baking sheet. Spread the zucchini halves with the ricotta mixture. Bake until golden brown.

Nutrition (for 100g): 200 Calories 12g Fat 3g Carbohydrates 11g Protein 836mg Sodium

Farro with Roasted Tomatoes and Mushrooms

Preparation Time : 20 minutes
Cooking Time : 1 hour
Servings : 4
Difficulty Level : Difficult

Ingredients:

- For the Tomatoes
- 2 pints cherry tomatoes
- 1 teaspoon extra-virgin olive oil
- ¼ teaspoon kosher salt
- For the Farro
- 3 to 4 cups water
- ½ cup farro
- ¼ teaspoon kosher salt
- For the Mushrooms
- 2 tablespoons extra-virgin olive oil
- 1 onion, julienned
- ½ teaspoon kosher salt
- ¼ teaspoon freshly ground black pepper
- 10 ounces baby bell mushrooms, stemmed and sliced thin
- ½ cup no-salt-added vegetable stock

- 1 (15-ounce) can low-sodium cannellini beans, drained and rinsed
- 1 cup baby spinach
- 2 tablespoons fresh basil, cut into ribbons
- ¼ cup pine nuts, toasted
- Aged balsamic vinegar (optional)

Directions:

To Make the Tomatoes

Preheat the oven to 400°F. Put parchment paper or foil into the baking sheet. Mix the tomatoes, olive oil, and salt together on the baking sheet and roast for 30 minutes.

To Make the Farro

Bring the water, farro, and salt to a boil in a medium saucepan or pot over high heat. Allow to simmer, and cook for 30 minutes, or until the farro is al dente. Drain and set aside.

To Make the Mushrooms

Cook the olive oil in a large skillet or sauté pan over medium-low heat. Add the onions, salt, and black pepper and sauté until golden brown and starting to caramelize, about 15 minutes. Stir in the mushrooms, increase the heat to medium, and sauté until the liquid has evaporated and the mushrooms brown, about 10 minutes. Stir in the vegetable stock and deglaze the pan, scraping up any brown bits, and reduce the liquid for about 5 minutes. Add the beans and warm through, about 3 minutes.

Remove and stir in the spinach, basil, pine nuts, roasted tomatoes, and farro. Dash with balsamic vinegar, if desired.

Nutrition (for 100g): 375 Calories 15g Fat 10g Carbohydrates 14g Protein 769mg Sodium

Baked Orzo with Eggplant, Swiss Chard, and Mozzarella

Preparation Time : 20 minutes
Cooking Time : 60 minutes
Servings : 4
Difficulty Level : Average

Ingredients:

- 2 tablespoons extra-virgin olive oil
- 1 large (1-pound) eggplant, diced small
- 2 carrots, peeled and diced small
- 2 celery stalks, diced small
- 1 onion, diced small
- ½ teaspoon kosher salt
- 3 garlic cloves, minced
- ¼ teaspoon freshly ground black pepper
- 1 cup whole-wheat orzo
- 1 teaspoon no-salt-added tomato paste
- 1½ cups no-salt-added vegetable stock
- 1 cup Swiss chard, stemmed and chopped small
- 2 tablespoons fresh oregano, chopped
- Zest of 1 lemon
- 4 ounces mozzarella cheese, diced small
- ¼ cup grated Parmesan cheese
- 2 tomatoes, sliced ½-inch-thick

Directions:

Preheat the oven to 400°F. Cook the olive oil in a large oven-safe sauté pan over medium heat. Add the eggplant, carrots, celery, onion, and salt and sauté about 10 minutes. Add the garlic and black pepper and sauté about 30 seconds. Add the orzo and tomato paste and sauté 1 minute. Mix in the vegetable stock and deglaze the pan, scraping up the brown bits. Add the Swiss chard, oregano, and lemon zest and stir until the chard wilts.

Pull out and put in the mozzarella cheese. Smooth the top of the orzo mixture flat. Sprinkle the Parmesan cheese over the top. Spread the tomatoes in a single layer on top of the Parmesan cheese. Bake for 45 minutes.

Nutrition (for 100g): 470 Calories 17g Fat 7g Carbohydrates 18g Protein 769mg Sodium

Barley Risotto with Tomatoes

Preparation Time : 20 minutes

Cooking Time : 45 minutes

Servings : 4

Difficulty Level : Average

Ingredients:

- 2 tablespoons extra-virgin olive oil
- 2 celery stalks, diced
- ½ cup shallots, diced
- 4 garlic cloves, minced
- 3 cups no-salt-added vegetable stock
- 1 (14.5-ounce) can no-salt-added diced tomatoes
- 1 (14.5-ounce) can no-salt-added crushed tomatoes
- 1 cup pearl barley
- Zest of 1 lemon
- 1 teaspoon kosher salt
- ½ teaspoon smoked paprika
- ¼ teaspoon red pepper flakes
- ¼ teaspoon freshly ground black pepper
- 4 thyme sprigs
- 1 dried bay leaf
- 2 cups baby spinach
- ½ cup crumbled feta cheese
- 1 tablespoon fresh oregano, chopped

- 1 tablespoon fennel seeds, toasted (optional)

Directions:

Cook the olive oil in a large saucepan over medium heat. Add the celery and shallots and sauté, about 4 to 5 minutes. Add the garlic and sauté 30 seconds. Add the vegetable stock, diced tomatoes, crushed tomatoes, barley, lemon zest, salt, paprika, red pepper flakes, black pepper, thyme, and the bay leaf, and mix well. Let it boil, then lower to low, and simmer. Cook, stirring occasionally, for 40 minutes.

Remove the bay leaf and thyme sprigs. Stir in the spinach. In a small bowl, combine the feta, oregano, and fennel seeds. Serve the barley risotto in bowls topped with the feta mixture.

Nutrition (for 100g): 375 Calories 12g Fat 13g Carbohydrates 11g Protein 799mg Sodium

Chickpeas and Kale with Spicy Pomodoro Sauce

Preparation Time : 10 minutes
Cooking Time : 35 minutes
Servings : 4
Difficulty Level : Easy

Ingredients:

- 2 tablespoons extra-virgin olive oil
- 4 garlic cloves, sliced
- 1 teaspoon red pepper flakes
- 1 (28-ounce) can no-salt-added crushed tomatoes
- 1 teaspoon kosher salt
- ½ teaspoon honey
- 1 bunch kale, stemmed and chopped
- 2 (15-ounce) cans low-sodium chickpeas, drained and rinsed
- ¼ cup fresh basil, chopped
- ¼ cup grated pecorino Romano cheese

Directions:

Cook the olive oil in a sauté pan over medium heat. Stir in the garlic and red pepper flakes and sauté until the garlic is a light golden brown, about 2 minutes. Add the tomatoes, salt, and honey and mix well. Reduce the heat to low and simmer for 20 minutes.

Add the kale and mix in well. Cook about 5 minutes. Add the chickpeas and simmer about 5 minutes. Remove from heat and stir in the basil. Serve topped with pecorino cheese.

Nutrition (for 100g): 420 Calories 13g Fat 12g Carbohydrates 20g Protein 882mg Sodium

Roasted Feta with Kale and Lemon Yogurt

Preparation Time : 15 minutes

Cooking Time : 20 minutes

Servings : 4

Difficulty Level : Average

Ingredients:

- 1 tablespoon extra-virgin olive oil
- 1 onion, julienned
- ¼ teaspoon kosher salt
- 1 teaspoon ground turmeric
- ½ teaspoon ground cumin
- ½ teaspoon ground coriander
- ¼ teaspoon freshly ground black pepper
- 1 bunch kale, stemmed and chopped
- 7-ounce block feta cheese, cut into ¼-inch-thick slices
- ½ cup plain Greek yogurt
- 1 tablespoon lemon juice

Directions:

Preheat the oven to 400°F. Fry the olive oil in a large ovenproof skillet or sauté pan over medium heat. Add the onion and salt; sauté until lightly golden brown, about 5 minutes. Add the turmeric, cumin, coriander, and black pepper; sauté for 30 seconds. Add the kale and sauté about 2 minutes. Add ½ cup water and continue to cook down the kale, about 3 minutes.

Remove from the heat and place the feta cheese slices on top of the kale mixture. Introduce in the oven and bake until the feta softens, 10 to 12 minutes. In a small bowl, combine the yogurt and lemon juice. Serve the kale and feta cheese topped with the lemon yogurt.

Nutrition (for 100g): 210 Calories 14g Fat 2g Carbohydrates 11g Protein 836mg Sodium

Roasted Eggplant and Chickpeas with Tomato Sauce

Preparation Time : 15 minutes

Cooking Time : 60 minutes

Servings : 4

Difficulty Level : Difficult

Ingredients:

- Olive oil cooking spray
- 1 large (about 1 pound) eggplant, sliced into ¼-inch-thick rounds
- 1 teaspoon kosher salt, divided
- 1 tablespoon extra-virgin olive oil
- 3 garlic cloves, minced
- 1 (28-ounce) can no-salt-added crushed tomatoes
- ½ teaspoon honey
- ¼ teaspoon freshly ground black pepper
- 2 tablespoons fresh basil, chopped
- 1 (15-ounce) can no-salt-added or low-sodium chickpeas, drained and rinsed
- ¾ cup crumbled feta cheese
- 1 tablespoon fresh oregano, chopped

Directions:

Preheat the oven to 425°F. Grease and line two baking sheets with foil and lightly spray with olive oil cooking spray. Spread the eggplant in a single layer and sprinkle with ½ teaspoon of the salt. Bake for 20 minutes, turning once halfway, until lightly golden brown.

Meanwhile, heat the olive oil in a large saucepan over medium heat. Mix in the garlic and sauté for 30 seconds. Add the crushed tomatoes, honey, the remaining ½ teaspoon salt, and black pepper. Simmer about 20 minutes, until the sauce reduces a bit and thickens. Stir in the basil.

After removing the eggplant from the oven, reduce the oven temperature to 375°F. In a large rectangular or oval baking dish, spoon in the chickpeas and 1 cup sauce. Layer the eggplant slices on top, overlapping as necessary to cover the chickpeas. Lay the remaining sauce on top of the eggplant. Sprinkle the feta cheese and oregano on top.

Wrap the baking dish with foil and bake for 15 minutes. Pull out the foil and bake an additional 15 minutes.

Nutrition (for 100g): 320 Calories 11g Fat 12g Carbohydrates 14g Protein 773mg Sodium

Baked Falafel Sliders

Preparation Time : 10 minutes

Cooking Time : 30 minutes

Servings : 6

Difficulty Level : Average

Ingredients:

- Olive oil cooking spray
- 1 (15-ounce) can low-sodium chickpeas, drained and rinsed
- 1 onion, roughly chopped
- 2 garlic cloves, peeled
- 2 tablespoons fresh parsley, chopped
- 2 tablespoons whole-wheat flour
- ½ teaspoon ground coriander
- ½ teaspoon ground cumin
- ½ teaspoon baking powder
- ½ teaspoon kosher salt
- ¼ teaspoon freshly ground black pepper

Directions:

Preheat the oven to 350°F. Put parchment paper or foil and lightly spray with olive oil cooking spray in the baking sheet.

In a food processor, mix in the chickpeas, onion, garlic, parsley, flour, coriander, cumin, baking powder, salt, and black pepper. Blend until smooth.

Make 6 slider patties, each with a heaping ¼ cup of mixture, and arrange on the prepared baking sheet. Bake for 30 minutes. Serve.

Nutrition (for 100g): 90 Calories 1g Fat 3g Carbohydrates 4g Protein 803mg Sodium

Portobello Caprese

Preparation Time : 15 minutes

Cooking Time : 30 minutes

Servings : 2

Difficulty Level : Difficult

Ingredients:

- 1 tablespoon olive oil
- 1 cup cherry tomatoes
- Salt and black pepper, to taste
- 4 large fresh basil leaves, thinly sliced, divided
- 3 medium garlic cloves, minced
- 2 large portobello mushrooms, stems removed
- 4 pieces mini Mozzarella balls
- 1 tablespoon Parmesan cheese, grated

Directions:

Prepare the oven to 350°F (180ºC). Grease a baking pan with olive oil. Drizzle 1 tablespoon olive oil in a nonstick skillet, and heat over medium-high heat. Add the tomatoes to the skillet, and sprinkle salt and black pepper to season. Prick some holes on the tomatoes for juice during the cooking. Put the lid on and cook the tomatoes for 10 minutes or until tender.

Reserve 2 teaspoons of basil and add the remaining basil and garlic to the skillet. Crush the tomatoes with a spatula, then cook for half a minute. Stir constantly during the cooking. Set aside. Arrange the mushrooms in the baking pan, cap side down, and sprinkle with salt and black pepper to taste.

Spoon the tomato mixture and Mozzarella balls on the gill of the mushrooms, then scatter with Parmesan cheese to coat well. Bake until the mushrooms are fork-tender and the cheeses are browned. Pull out the stuffed mushrooms from the oven and serve with basil on top.

Nutrition (for 100g): 285 Calories 21.8g Fat 2.1g Carbohydrates 14.3g Protein 823mg Sodium

Mushroom and Cheese Stuffed Tomatoes

Preparation Time : 15 minutes

Cooking Time : 20 minutes

Servings : 4

Difficulty Level : Average

Ingredients:

- 4 large ripe tomatoes
- 1 tablespoon olive oil
- ½ pound (454 g) white or cremini mushrooms, sliced
- 1 tablespoon fresh basil, chopped
- ½ cup yellow onion, diced
- 1 tablespoon fresh oregano, chopped
- 2 garlic cloves, minced
- ½ teaspoon salt
- ¼ teaspoon freshly ground black pepper
- 1 cup part-skim Mozzarella cheese, shredded
- 1 tablespoon Parmesan cheese, grated

Directions:

Ready the oven to 375°F (190°C). Cut a ½-inch slice off the top of each tomato. Scoop the pulp into a bowl and leave ½-inch tomato shells. Arrange the tomatoes on a baking sheet lined with aluminum foil. Heat the olive oil in a nonstick skillet over medium heat.

Add the mushrooms, basil, onion, oregano, garlic, salt, and black pepper to the skillet and sauté for 5 minutes.

Pour the mixture to the tomato pulp bowl, then add the Mozzarella cheese and stir to combine well. Spoon the mixture into each tomato shell, then top with a layer of Parmesan. Bake in the preheated oven for 15 minutes or until the cheese is bubbly and the tomatoes are soft. Pull out the stuffed tomatoes from the oven and serve warm.

Nutrition (for 100g): 254 Calories 14.7g Fat 5.2g Carbohydrates 17.5g Protein 783mg Sodium

Tabbouleh

Preparation Time : 15 minutes

Cooking Time : 5 minutes

Servings : 6

Difficulty Level : Average

Ingredients:

- 4 tablespoons olive oil, divided
- 4 cups riced cauliflower
- 3 garlic cloves, finely minced
- Salt and black pepper, to taste
- ½ large cucumber, peeled, seeded, and chopped
- ½ cup Italian parsley, chopped
- Juice of 1 lemon
- 2 tablespoons minced red onion
- ½ cup mint leaves, chopped
- ½ cup pitted Kalamata olives, chopped
- 1 cup cherry tomatoes, quartered
- 2 cups baby arugula or spinach leaves
- 2 medium avocados, peeled, pitted, and diced

Directions:

Warm 2 tablespoons olive oil in a nonstick skillet over medium-high heat. Add the rice cauliflower, garlic, salt, and black pepper to the skillet and sauté for 3 minutes or until fragrant. Transfer them to a large bowl.

Add the cucumber, parsley, lemon juice, red onion, mint, olives, and remaining olive oil to the bowl. Toss to combine well. Reserve the bowl in the refrigerator for at least 30 minutes.

Remove the bowl from the refrigerator. Add the cherry tomatoes, arugula, avocado to the bowl. Season well, and toss to combine well. Serve chilled.

Nutrition (for 100g): 198 Calories 17.5g Fat 6.2g Carbohydrates 4.2g Protein 773mg Sodium

Spicy Broccoli Rabe And Artichoke Hearts

Preparation Time : 5 minutes

Cooking Time : 15 minutes

Servings : 4

Difficulty Level : Average

Ingredients:

- 3 tablespoons olive oil, divided
- 2 pounds (907 g) fresh broccoli rabe
- 3 garlic cloves, finely minced
- 1 teaspoon red pepper flakes
- 1 teaspoon salt, plus more to taste
- 13.5 ounces (383 g) artichoke hearts
- 1 tablespoon water
- 2 tablespoons red wine vinegar
- Freshly ground black pepper, to taste

Directions:

Warm 2 tablespoons olive oil in a nonstick skillet over medium-high skillet. Add the broccoli, garlic, red pepper flakes, and salt to the skillet and sauté for 5 minutes or until the broccoli is soft.

Put the artichoke hearts to the skillet and sauté for 2 more minutes or until tender. Add water to the skillet and turn down the heat to low. Put the lid on and simmer for 5 minutes. Meanwhile, combine the vinegar and 1 tablespoon of olive oil in a bowl.

Drizzle the simmered broccoli and artichokes with oiled vinegar, and sprinkle with salt and black pepper. Toss to combine well before serving.

Nutrition (for 100g): 272 Calories 21.5g Fat 9.8g Carbohydrates 11.2g Protein 736mg Sodium

Shakshuka

Preparation Time : 10 minutes

Cooking Time : 25 minutes

Servings : 4

Difficulty Level : Difficult

Ingredients:

- 5 tablespoons olive oil, divided
- 1 red bell pepper, finely diced
- ½ small yellow onion, finely diced
- 14 ounces (397 g) crushed tomatoes, with juices
- 6 ounces (170 g) frozen spinach, thawed and drained of excess liquid
- 1 teaspoon smoked paprika
- 2 garlic cloves, finely minced
- 2 teaspoons red pepper flakes
- 1 tablespoon capers, roughly chopped
- 1 tablespoon water
- 6 large eggs
- ¼ teaspoon freshly ground black pepper
- ¾ cup feta or goat cheese, crumbled
- ¼ cup fresh flat-leaf parsley or cilantro, chopped

Directions:

Ready the oven to 300ºF (150ºC). Heat 2 tablespoons olive oil in an oven-safe skillet over medium-high heat. Sauté the bell pepper and onion to the skillet until the onion is translucent and the bell pepper is soft.

Add the tomatoes and juices, spinach, paprika, garlic, red pepper flakes, capers, water, and 2 tablespoons olive oil to the skillet. Stir well and bring to a boil. Set down the heat to low, then put the lid on and simmer for 5 minutes.

Crack the eggs over the sauce, keep a little space between each egg, leave the egg intact and sprinkle with freshly ground black pepper. Cook until the eggs reach the right doneness.

Scatter the cheese over the eggs and sauce, and bake in the preheated oven for 5 minutes or until the cheese is frothy and golden brown. Drizzle with the remaining 1 tablespoon olive oil and spread the parsley on top before serving warm.

Nutrition (for 100g): 335 Calories 26.5g Fat 5g Carbohydrates 16.8g Protein 736mg Sodium

Spanakopita

Preparation Time : 15 minutes

Cooking Time : 50 minutes

Servings : 6

Difficulty Level : Difficult

Ingredients:

- 6 tablespoons olive oil, divided
- 1 small yellow onion, diced
- 4 cups frozen chopped spinach
- 4 garlic cloves, minced
- ½ teaspoon salt
- ½ teaspoon freshly ground black pepper
- 4 large eggs, beaten
- 1 cup ricotta cheese
- ¾ cup feta cheese, crumbled
- ¼ cup pine nuts

Directions:

Grease baking dish with 2 tablespoons olive oil. Organize the oven at 375 degrees F. Heat 2 tablespoons olive oil in a nonstick skillet over medium-high heat. Mix in the onion to the skillet and sauté for 6 minutes or until translucent and tender.

Add the spinach, garlic, salt, and black pepper to the skillet and sauté for 5 minutes more. Place them to a bowl and set aside.

Combine the beaten eggs and ricotta cheese in a separate bowl, then pour them in to the bowl of spinach mixture. Stir to mix well.

Fill the mixture into the baking dish, and tilt the dish so the mixture coats the bottom evenly. Bake until it begins to set. Take out the baking dish from the oven, and spread the feta cheese and pine nuts on top, then dash with remaining 2 tablespoons olive oil.

Return the baking dish to the oven and bake for another 15 minutes or until the top is golden brown. Remove the dish from the oven. Allow the spanakopita to cool for a few minutes and slice to serve.

Nutrition (for 100g): 340 Calories 27.3g Fat 10.1g Carbohydrates 18.2g Protein 781mg Sodium

Tagine

Preparation Time : 20 minutes
Cooking Time : 60 minutes
Servings : 6
Difficulty Level : Average

Ingredients:

- ½ cup olive oil
- 6 celery stalks, sliced into ¼-inch crescents
- 2 medium yellow onions, sliced
- 1 teaspoon ground cumin
- ½ teaspoon ground cinnamon
- 1 teaspoon ginger powder
- 6 garlic cloves, minced
- ½ teaspoon paprika
- 1 teaspoon salt
- ¼ teaspoon freshly ground black pepper
- 2 cups low-sodium vegetable stock
- 2 medium zucchinis, cut into ½-inch-thick semicircles
- 2 cups cauliflower, cut into florets
- 1 medium eggplant, cut into 1-inch cubes
- 1 cup green olives, halved and pitted
- 13.5 ounces (383 g) artichoke hearts, drained and quartered
- ½ cup chopped fresh cilantro leaves, for garnish
- ½ cup plain Greek yogurt, for garnish

- ½ cup chopped fresh flat-leaf parsley, for garnish

Directions:

Cook the olive oil in a stockpot over medium-high heat. Add the celery and onion to the pot and sauté for 6 minutes. Put the cumin, cinnamon, ginger, garlic, paprika, salt, and black pepper to the pot and sauté for 2 minutes more until aromatic.

Pour the vegetable stock to the pot and bring to a boil. Turn down the heat to low, and add the zucchini, cauliflower, and eggplant to the bank. Cover and simmer for 30 minutes or until the vegetables are soft. Then add the olives and artichoke hearts to the pool and simmer for 15 minutes more. Fill them into a large serving bowl or a Tagine, then serve with cilantro, Greek yogurt, and parsley on top.

Nutrition (for 100g): 312 Calories 21.2g Fat 9.2g Carbohydrates 6.1g Protein 813mg Sodium

Citrus Pistachios and Asparagus

Preparation Time : 10 minutes

Cooking Time : 10 minutes

Servings : 4

Difficulty Level : Difficult

Ingredients:

- Zest and juice of 2 clementine or 1 orange
- Zest and juice of 1 lemon
- 1 tablespoon red wine vinegar
- 3 tablespoons extra-virgin olive oil, divided
- 1 teaspoon salt, divided
- ¼ teaspoon freshly ground black pepper
- ½ cup pistachios, shelled
- 1 pound (454 g) fresh asparagus, trimmed
- 1 tablespoon water

Directions:

Combine the zest and juice of clementine and lemon, vinegar, 2 tablespoons of olive oil, ½ teaspoon of salt, and black pepper. Stir to mix well. Set aside.

Toast the pistachios in a nonstick skillet over medium-high heat for 2 minutes or until golden brown. Transfer the roasted pistachios to a clean work surface, then chop roughly. Mix the pistachios with the citrus mixture. Set aside.

Heat the remaining olive oil in the nonstick skillet over medium-high heat. Add the asparagus to the skillet and sauté for 2 minutes, then season with remaining salt. Add the water to the skillet. Put down the heat to low, and put the lid on. Simmer for 4 minutes until the asparagus is tender.

Remove the asparagus from the skillet to a large dish. Pour the citrus and pistachios mixture over the asparagus. Toss to coat well before serving.

Nutrition (for 100g): 211 Calories 17.5g Fat 3.8g Carbohydrates 5.9g Protein 901mg Sodium

Tomato and Parsley Stuffed Eggplant

Preparation Time : 15 minutes

Cooking Time : 2 hours and 10 minutes

Servings : 6

Difficulty Level : Average

Ingredients:

- ¼ cup extra-virgin olive oil
- 3 small eggplants, cut in half lengthwise
- 1 teaspoon sea salt
- ½ teaspoon freshly ground black pepper
- 1 large yellow onion, finely chopped
- 4 garlic cloves, minced
- 15 ounces (425 g) diced tomatoes, with the juice
- ¼ cup fresh flat-leaf parsley, finely chopped

Directions:

Put the insert of the slow cooker with 2 tablespoons of olive oil. Cut some slits on the cut side of each eggplant half, keep a ¼-inch space between each slit. Place the eggplant halves in the slow cooker, skin side down. Sprinkle with salt and black pepper.

Warm up the remaining olive oil in a nonstick skillet over medium-high heat. Add the onion and garlic to the skillet and sauté for 3 minutes or until the onion is translucent.

Add the parsley and tomatoes with the juice to the skillet, and sprinkle with salt and black pepper. Sauté for 5 more minutes or until they are tender. Divide and spoon the mixture in the skillet on the eggplant halves.

Situate the slow cooker lid on and cook on HIGH for 2 hours until the eggplant is soft. Transfer the eggplant to a plate, and allow to cool for a few minutes before serving.

Nutrition (for 100g): 455 Calories 13g Fat 14g Carbohydrates 14g Protein 719mg Sodium

Ratatouille

Preparation Time : 15 minutes

Cooking Time : 7 hours

Servings : 6

Difficulty Level : Average

Ingredients:

- 3 tablespoons extra-virgin olive oil
- 1 large eggplant, unpeeled, sliced
- 2 large onions, sliced
- 4 small zucchinis, sliced
- 2 green bell peppers
- 6 large tomatoes, cut in ½-inch wedges
- 2 tablespoons fresh flat-leaf parsley, chopped
- 1 teaspoon dried basil
- 2 garlic cloves, minced
- 2 teaspoons sea salt
- ¼ teaspoon freshly ground black pepper

Direction:

Fill the insert of the slow cooker with 2 tablespoons olive oil. Arrange the vegetables slices, strips, and wedges alternately in the insert of the slow cooker. Spread the parsley on top of the vegetables, and season with basil, garlic, salt, and black pepper. Drizzle with the remaining olive oil. Close and cook on LOW for 7 hours until the vegetables are tender. Transfer the vegetables on a plate and serve warm.

Nutrition (for 100g): 265 Calories 1.7g Fat 13.7g Carbohydrates 8.3g Protein 800mg Sodium

Gemista

Preparation Time : 15 minutes

Cooking Time : 4 hours

Servings : 4

Difficulty Level : Average

Ingredients:

- 2 tablespoons extra-virgin olive oil
- 4 large bell peppers, any color
- ½ cup uncooked couscous
- 1 teaspoon oregano
- 1 garlic clove, minced
- 1 cup crumbled feta cheese
- 1 (15-ounce / 425-g) can cannellini beans, rinsed and drained
- Salt and pepper, to taste
- 1 lemon wedges
- 4 green onions, white and green parts separated, thinly sliced

Direction:

Cut a ½-inch slice below the stem from the top of the bell pepper. Discard the stem only and chop the sliced top portion under the stem, and reserve in a bowl. Hollow the bell pepper with a spoon. Grease the slow cooker with oil.

Incorporate the remaining ingredients, except for the green parts of the green onion and lemon wedges, to the bowl of chopped bell pepper top. Stir to mix well. Spoon the mixture in the hollowed bell pepper, and arrange the stuffed bell peppers in the slow cooker, then drizzle with more olive oil.

Seal the slow cooker lid on and cook on HIGH for 4 hours or until the bell peppers are soft.

Remove the bell peppers from the slow cooker and serve on a plate. Sprinkle with green parts of the green onions, and squeeze the lemon wedges on top before serving.

Nutrition (for 100g): 246 Calories 9g Fat 6.5g Carbohydrates 11.1g Protein 698mg Sodium

Stuffed Cabbage Rolls

Preparation Time : 15 minutes

Cooking Time : 2 hours

Servings : 4

Difficulty Level : Difficult

Ingredients:

- 4 tablespoons olive oil, divided
- 1 large head green cabbage, cored
- 1 large yellow onion, chopped
- 3 ounces (85 g) feta cheese, crumbled
- ½ cup dried currants
- 3 cups cooked pearl barley
- 2 tablespoons fresh flat-leaf parsley, chopped
- 2 tablespoons pine nuts, toasted
- ½ teaspoon sea salt
- ½ teaspoon black pepper
- 15 ounces (425 g) crushed tomatoes, with the juice
- 1 tablespoon apple cider vinegar
- ½ cup apple juice

Directions:

Brush off the insert of the slow cooker with 2 tablespoons olive oil. Blanch the cabbage in a pot of water for 8 minutes. Take it from the water, and set aside, then separate 16 leaves from the cabbage. Set aside.

Drizzle the remaining olive oil in a nonstick skillet, and heat over medium heat. Stir in the onion to the skillet and cook until the onion and bell pepper is tender. Transfer the onion to a bowl.

Add the feta cheese, currants, barley, parsley, and pine nuts to the bowl of cooked onion, then sprinkle with ¼ teaspoon of salt and ¼ teaspoon of black pepper.

Arrange the cabbage leaves on a clean work surface. Scoop 1/3 cup of the mixture on the center of each plate, then fold the edge onto the mixture and roll it up. Place the cabbage rolls in the slow cooker, seam side down.

Incorporate the remaining ingredients in a separate bowl, then pour the mixture over the cabbage rolls. Seal slow cooker lid on and cook on HIGH for 2 hours. Remove the cabbage rolls from the slow cooker and serve warm.

Nutrition (for 100g): 383 Calories 14.7g Fat 12.9g Carbohydrates 10.7g Protein 838mg Sodium

Brussels Sprouts with Balsamic Glaze

Preparation Time : 15 minutes

Cooking Time : 2 hours

Servings : 6

Difficulty Level : Average

Ingredients:

- Balsamic Glaze:
- 1 cup balsamic vinegar
- ¼ cup honey
- 2 tablespoons extra-virgin olive oil
- 2 pounds (907 g) Brussels sprouts, trimmed and halved
- 2 cups low-sodium vegetable soup
- 1 teaspoon sea salt
- Freshly ground black pepper, to taste
- ¼ cup Parmesan cheese, grated
- ¼ cup pine nuts

Directions:

Make the balsamic glaze: Combine the balsamic vinegar and honey in a saucepan. Stir to mix well. Over medium-high heat, bring to a boil. Set down the heat to low, then simmer for 20 minutes or until the glaze reduces in half and has a thick consistency. Impose some olive oil inside the insert of the slow cooker.

Put the Brussels sprouts, vegetable soup, and ½ teaspoon of salt in the slow cooker, stir to combine. Seal the slow cooker lid on and cook on HIGH for 2 hours until the Brussels sprouts are soft.

Put the Brussels sprouts to a plate, and sprinkle the remaining salt and black pepper to season. Dash the balsamic glaze over the Brussels sprouts, then serve with Parmesan and pine nuts.

Nutrition (for 100g): 270 Calories 10.6g Fat 6.9g Carbohydrates 8.7g Protein 693mg Sodium

Spinach Salad with Citrus Vinaigrette

Preparation Time : 10 minutes

Cooking Time : 0 minutes

Servings : 4

Difficulty Level : Easy

Ingredients:

- Citrus Vinaigrette:
- ¼ cup extra-virgin olive oil
- 3 tablespoons balsamic vinegar
- ½ teaspoon fresh lemon zest
- ½ teaspoon salt
- Salad:
- 1-pound (454 g) baby spinach, washed, stems removed
- 1 large ripe tomato, cut into ¼-inch pieces
- 1 medium red onion, thinly sliced

Directions:

Make the citrus vinaigrette: Stir together the olive oil, balsamic vinegar, lemon zest, and salt in a bowl until mixed well.

Make the salad: Place the baby spinach, tomato and onions in a separate salad bowl. Fill the citrus vinaigrette over the salad and gently toss until the vegetables are coated thoroughly.

Nutrition (for 100g): 173 Calories 14.2g Fat 4.2g Carbohydrates 4.1g Protein 699mg Sodium

Simple Celery and Orange Salad

Preparation Time : 15 minutes

Cooking Time : 0 minutes

Servings : 6

Difficulty Level : Easy

Ingredients:

- <u>Salad:</u>
- 3 celery stalks, including leaves, sliced diagonally into ½-inch slices
- ½ cup green olives
- ¼ cup sliced red onion
- 2 large peeled oranges, cut into rounds
- <u>Dressing:</u>
- 1 tablespoon extra-virgin olive oil
- 1 tablespoon lemon or orange juice
- 1 tablespoon olive brine
- ¼ teaspoon kosher or sea salt
- ¼ teaspoon freshly ground black pepper

Directions:

Make the salad: Put the celery stalks, green olives, onion, and oranges in a shallow bowl. Mix well and set aside.

Make the dressing: Stir the olive oil, lemon juice, olive brine, salt, and pepper well.

Fill the dressing into the bowl of salad and lightly toss until coated thoroughly.

Serve chilled or at room temperature.

Nutrition (for 100g): 24 Calories 1.2g Fat 1.2g Carbohydrates 1.1g Protein 813mg Sodium

Fried Eggplant Rolls

Preparation Time : 20 minutes

Cooking Time : 10 minutes

Servings : 6

Difficulty Level : Average

Ingredients:

- 2 large eggplants
- 1 teaspoon salt
- 1 cup shredded ricotta cheese
- 4 ounces (113 g) goat cheese, shredded
- ¼ cup finely chopped fresh basil
- ½ teaspoon freshly ground black pepper
- Olive oil spray

Directions:

Add the eggplant slices to a colander and season with salt. Set aside for 15 to 20 minutes.

Mix together the ricotta and goat cheese, basil, and black pepper in a large bowl and stir to combine. Set aside. Pat dry the eggplant slices with paper towels and lightly mist them with olive oil spray.

Warm up large skillet over medium heat and lightly spray it with olive oil spray. Arrange the eggplant slices in the skillet and fry each side for 3 minutes until golden brown.

Remove from the heat to a paper towel-lined plate and rest for 5 minutes. Make the eggplant rolls: Lay the eggplant slices on a flat work surface and top each slice with a tablespoon of the prepared cheese mixture. Roll them up and serve immediately.

Nutrition (for 100g): 254 Calories 14.9g Fat 7.1g Carbohydrates 15.3g Protein 612mg Sodium

Roasted Veggies and Brown Rice Bowl

Preparation Time : 15 minutes

Cooking Time : 20 minutes

Servings : 4

Difficulty Level : Average

Ingredients:

- 2 cups cauliflower florets
- 2 cups broccoli florets
- 1 (15-ounce / 425-g) can chickpeas
- 1 cup carrot slices (about 1 inch thick)
- 2 to 3 tablespoons extra-virgin olive oil, divided
- Salt and black pepper, to taste
- Nonstick cooking spray
- 2 cups cooked brown rice
- 3 tablespoons sesame seeds
- <u>Dressing:</u>
- 3 to 4 tablespoons tahini
- 2 tablespoons honey
- 1 lemon, juiced
- 1 garlic clove, minced
- Salt and black pepper, to taste

Directions:

Ready the oven to 400ºF (205ºC). Spritz two baking sheets with nonstick cooking spray.

Spread the cauliflower and broccoli on the first baking sheet and the second with the chickpeas and carrot slices.

Drizzle each sheet with half of the olive oil and sprinkle with salt and pepper. Toss to coat well.

Roast the chickpeas and carrot slices in the preheated oven for 10 minutes, leaving the carrots tender but crisp, and the cauliflower and broccoli for 20 minutes until fork-tender. Stir them once halfway through the cooking time.

Meanwhile, make the dressing: Whisk together the tahini, honey, lemon juice, garlic, salt, and pepper in a small bowl.

Divide the cooked brown rice among four bowls. Top each bowl evenly with roasted vegetables and dressing. Sprinkle the sesame seeds on top for garnish before serving.

Nutrition (for 100g): 453 Calories 17.8g Fat 11.2g Carbohydrates 12.1g Protein 793mg Sodium

Cauliflower Hash with Carrots

Preparation Time : 10 minutes

Cooking Time : 10 minutes

Servings : 4

Difficulty Level : Easy

Ingredients:

- 3 tablespoons extra-virgin olive oil
- 1 large onion, chopped
- 1 tablespoon minced garlic
- 2 cups diced carrots
- 4 cups cauliflower florets
- ½ teaspoon ground cumin
- 1 teaspoon salt

Directions:

Cook the olive oil over medium heat. Mix in the onion and garlic and sauté for 1 minute. Stir in the carrots and stir-fry for 3 minutes. Add the cauliflower florets, cumin, and salt and toss to combine.

Cover and cook for 3 minutes until lightly browned. Stir well and cook, uncovered, for 3 to 4 minutes, until softened. Remove from the heat and serve warm.

Nutrition (for 100g): 158 Calories 10.8g Fat 5.1g Carbohydrates 3.1g Protein 813mg Sodium

Garlicky Zucchini Cubes with Mint

Preparation Time : 5 minutes

Cooking Time : 10 minutes

Servings : 4

Difficulty Level : Easy

Ingredients:

- 3 large green zucchinis
- 3 tablespoons extra-virgin olive oil
- 1 large onion, chopped
- 3 cloves garlic, minced
- 1 teaspoon salt
- 1 teaspoon dried mint

Directions:

Cook the olive oil in a large skillet over medium heat.

Mix in the onion and garlic and sauté for 3 minutes, stirring constantly, or until softened.

Stir in the zucchini cubes and salt and cook for 5 minutes, or until the zucchini is browned and tender.

Add the mint to the skillet and toss to combine, then continue cooking for 2 minutes. Serve warm.

Nutrition (for 100g): 146 Calories 10.6g Fat 3g Carbohydrates 4.2g Protein 789mg Sodium

Zucchini and Artichokes Bowl with Faro

Preparation Time : 15 minutes

Cooking Time : 10 minutes

Servings : 6

Difficulty Level : Easy

Ingredients:

- 1/3 cup extra-virgin olive oil
- 1/3 cup chopped red onions
- ½ cup chopped red bell pepper
- 2 garlic cloves, minced
- 1 cup zucchini, cut into ½-inch-thick slices
- ½ cup coarsely chopped artichokes
- ½ cup canned chickpeas, drained and rinsed
- 3 cups cooked faro
- Salt and black pepper, to taste
- ½ cup crumbled feta cheese, for serving (optional)
- ¼ cup sliced olives, for serving (optional)
- 2 tablespoons fresh basil, chiffonade, for serving (optional)
- 3 tablespoons balsamic vinegar, for serving (optional)

Directions:

Heat up the olive oil in a large skillet over medium heat until it shimmers. Mix the onions, bell pepper, and garlic and sauté for 5 minutes, stirring occasionally, until softened.

Stir in the zucchini slices, artichokes, and chickpeas and sauté for about 5 minutes until slightly tender. Add the cooked faro and toss to combine until heated through. Sprinkle the salt and pepper to season.

Divide the mixture into bowls. Top each bowl evenly with feta cheese, olive slices, and basil and sprinkle with the balsamic vinegar, if desired.

Nutrition (for 100g): 366 Calories 19.9g Fat 9g Carbohydrates 9.3g Protein 819mg Sodium

5-Ingredient Zucchini Fritters

Preparation Time : 15 minutes

Cooking Time : 5 minutes

Servings : 14

Difficulty Level : Average

Ingredients:

- 4 cups grated zucchini
- Salt, to taste
- 2 large eggs, slightly beaten
- 1/3 cup sliced scallions
- 2/3 all-purpose flour
- 1/8 teaspoon black pepper
- 2 tablespoons olive oil

Directions:

Situate the grated zucchini in a colander and lightly season with salt. Set aside to rest for 10 minutes. Grip as much liquid from the grated zucchini as possible.

Pour the grated zucchini into a bowl. Fold in the beaten eggs, scallions, flour, salt, and pepper and stir until everything is well combined.

Heat up the olive oil in a large skillet over medium heat until hot.

Drop 3 tablespoons mounds of the zucchini mixture onto the hot skillet to make each fritter, pin them lightly into rounds and spacing them about 2 inches apart.

Cook for 2 to 3 minutes. Flip the zucchini fritters and cook for 2 minutes more, or until they are golden brown and cooked through.

Remove from the heat to a plate lined with paper towels. Repeat with the remaining zucchini mixture. Serve hot.

Nutrition (for 100g): 113 Calories 6.1g Fat 9g Carbohydrates 4g Protein 793mg Sodium

Moroccan Tagine with Vegetables

Preparation Time : 20 minutes

Cooking Time : 40 minutes

Servings : 2

Difficulty Level : Average

Ingredients:

- 2 tablespoons olive oil
- ½ onion, diced
- 1 garlic clove, minced
- 2 cups cauliflower florets
- 1 medium carrot, cut into 1-inch pieces
- 1 cup diced eggplant
- 1 can whole tomatoes with juices
- 1 (15-ounce / 425-g) can chickpeas
- 2 small red potatoes
- 1 cup water
- 1 teaspoon pure maple syrup
- ½ teaspoon cinnamon
- ½ teaspoon turmeric
- 1 teaspoon cumin
- ½ teaspoon salt
- 1 to 2 teaspoons harissa paste

Directions:

In a Dutch oven, heat up the olive oil over medium-high heat. Sauté the onion for 5 minutes, stirring occasionally, or until the onion is translucent.

Stir in the garlic, cauliflower florets, carrot, eggplant, tomatoes, and potatoes. Mash tomatoes by using a wooden spoon into smaller pieces.

Add the chickpeas, water, maple syrup, cinnamon, turmeric, cumin, and salt and stir to incorporate. Let it boil

Once done, reduce the heat to medium-low. Stir in the harissa paste, cover, allow to simmer for about 40 minutes, or until the vegetables are softened. Taste and adjust seasoning as needed. Let it rest before serving.

Nutrition (for 100g): 293 Calories 9.9g Fat 12.1g Carbohydrates 11.2g Protein 811mg Sodium

Chickpea Lettuce Wraps with Celery

Preparation Time : 10 minutes

Cooking Time : 0 minutes

Servings : 4

Difficulty Level : Easy

Ingredients:

- 1 (15-ounce / 425-g) can low-sodium chickpeas
- 1 celery stalk, thinly sliced
- 2 tablespoons finely chopped red onion
- 2 tablespoons unsalted tahini
- 3 tablespoons honey mustard
- 1 tablespoon capers, undrained
- 12 butter lettuce leaves

Directions:

In a bowl, puree the chickpeas with a potato masher or the back of a fork until mostly smooth. Add the celery, red onion, tahini, honey mustard, and capers to the bowl and stir until well incorporated.

For each serving, place three overlapping lettuce leaves on a plate and top with ¼ of the mashed chickpea filling, then roll up. Repeat with the remaining lettuce leaves and chickpea mixture.

Nutrition (for 100g): 182 Calories 7.1g Fat 3g Carbohydrates 10.3g Protein 743mg Sodium

Grilled Vegetable Skewers

Preparation Time : 15 minutes

Cooking Time : 10 minutes

Servings : 4

Difficulty Level : Easy

Ingredients:

- 4 medium red onions, peeled and sliced into 6 wedges
- 4 medium zucchinis, cut into 1-inch-thick slices
- 2 beefsteak tomatoes, cut into quarters
- 4 red bell peppers
- 2 orange bell peppers
- 2 yellow bell peppers
- 2 tablespoons plus 1 teaspoon olive oil

Directions:

Preheat the grill to medium-high heat. Skewer the vegetables by alternating between red onion, zucchini, tomatoes, and the different colored bell peppers. Grease them with 2 tablespoons of olive oil.

Oil the grill grates with 1 teaspoon of olive oil and grill the vegetable skewers for 5 minutes. Flip the skewers and grill for 5 minutes more, or until they are cooked to your liking. Let the skewers cool for 5 minutes before serving.

Nutrition (for 100g): 115 Calories 3g Fat 4.7g Carbohydrates 3.5g Protein 647mg Sodium

Stuffed Portobello Mushroom with Tomatoes

Preparation Time : 10 minutes
Cooking Time : 15 minutes
Servings : 4
Difficulty Level : Average

Ingredients:

- 4 large portobello mushroom caps
- 3 tablespoons extra-virgin olive oil
- Salt and black pepper, to taste
- 4 sun-dried tomatoes
- 1 cup shredded mozzarella cheese, divided
- ½ to ¾ cup low-sodium tomato sauce

Directions:

Preheat the broiler on high. Lay the mushroom caps on a baking sheet and drizzle with olive oil. Sprinkle with salt and pepper. Broil for 1o minutes, flipping the mushroom caps halfway through, until browned on the top.

Remove from the broil. Spoon 1 tomato, 2 tablespoons of cheese, and 2 to 3 tablespoons of sauce onto each mushroom cap. Return the mushroom caps to the broiler and continue broiling for 2 to 3 minutes. Cool for 5 minutes before serving.

Nutrition (for 100g): 217 Calories 15.8g Fat 9g Carbohydrates 11.2g Protein 793mg Sodium

Wilted Dandelion Greens with Sweet Onion

Preparation Time : 15 minutes
Cooking Time : 15 minutes
Servings : 4
Difficulty Level : Easy

Ingredients:

- 1 tablespoon extra-virgin olive oil
- 2 garlic cloves, minced
- 1 Vidalia onion, thinly sliced
- ½ cup low-sodium vegetable broth
- 2 bunches dandelion greens, roughly chopped
- Freshly ground black pepper, to taste

Directions:

Heat up the olive oil in a large skillet over low heat. Add the garlic and onion and cook for 2 to 3 minutes, stirring occasionally, or until the onion is translucent.

Fold in the vegetable broth and dandelion greens and cook for 5 to 7 minutes until wilted, stirring frequently. Sprinkle with the black pepper and serve on a plate while warm.

Nutrition (for 100g): 81 Calories 3.9g Fat 4g Carbohydrates 3.2g Protein 693mg Sodium

Celery and Mustard Greens

Preparation Time : 10 minutes

Cooking Time : 15 minutes

Servings : 4

Difficulty Level : Average

Ingredients:

- ½ cup low-sodium vegetable broth
- 1 celery stalk, roughly chopped
- ½ sweet onion, chopped
- ½ large red bell pepper, thinly sliced
- 2 garlic cloves, minced
- 1 bunch mustard greens, roughly chopped

Directions:

Pour the vegetable broth into a large cast iron pan and bring it to a simmer over medium heat. Stir in the celery, onion, bell pepper, and garlic. Cook uncovered for about 3 to 5 minutes.

Add the mustard greens to the pan and stir well. Decrease heat and cook until the liquid is evaporated and the greens are wilted. Remove from the heat and serve warm.

Nutrition (for 100g): 39 Calories 3.1g Protein 6.8g Carbohydrates 3g Protein 736mg Sodium

Vegetable and Tofu Scramble

Preparation Time : 5 minutes

Cooking Time : 10 minutes

Servings : 2

Difficulty Level : Easy

Ingredients:

- 2 tablespoons extra-virgin olive oil
- ½ red onion, finely chopped
- 1 cup chopped kale
- 8 ounces (227 g) mushrooms, sliced
- 8 ounces (227 g) tofu, cut into pieces
- 2 garlic cloves, minced
- Pinch red pepper flakes
- ½ teaspoon sea salt
- 1/8 teaspoon freshly ground black pepper

Directions:

Cook the olive oil in a medium nonstick skillet over medium-high heat until shimmering. Add the onion, kale, and mushrooms to the skillet. Cook and stirring irregularly, or until the vegetables start to brown.

Add the tofu and stir-fry for 3 to 4 minutes until softened. Stir in the garlic, red pepper flakes, salt, and black pepper and cook for 30 seconds. Let it rest before serving.

Nutrition (for 100g): 233 Calories 15.9g Fat 2g Carbohydrates 13.4g Protein 733mg Sodium

Simple Zoodles

Preparation Time : 10 minutes

Cooking Time : 5 minutes

Servings : 2

Difficulty Level : Easy

Ingredients:

- 2 tablespoons avocado oil
- 2 medium zucchinis, spiralized
- ¼ teaspoon salt
- Freshly ground black pepper, to taste

Directions:

Warm up the avocado oil in a large skillet over medium heat until it shimmers. Add the zucchini noodles, salt, and black pepper to the skillet and toss to coat. Cook and stir continuously, until tender. Serve warm.

Nutrition (for 100g): 128 Calories 14g Fat 0.3g Carbohydrates 0.3g Protein 811mg Sodium

Lentil and Tomato Collard Wraps

Preparation Time : 15 minutes

Cooking Time : 0 minutes

Servings : 4

Difficulty Level : Easy

Ingredients:

- 2 cups cooked lentils
- 5 Roma tomatoes, diced
- ½ cup crumbled feta cheese
- 10 large fresh basil leaves, thinly sliced
- ¼ cup extra-virgin olive oil
- 1 tablespoon balsamic vinegar
- 2 garlic cloves, minced
- ½ teaspoon raw honey
- ½ teaspoon salt
- ¼ teaspoon freshly ground black pepper
- 4 large collard leaves, stems removed

Directions:

Combine the lentils, tomatoes, cheese, basil leaves, olive oil, vinegar, garlic, honey, salt, and black pepper and stir well.

Lay the collard leaves on a flat work surface. Spoon the equal-sized amounts of the lentil mixture onto the edges of the leaves. Roll them up and slice in half to serve.

Nutrition (for 100g): 318 Calories 17.6g Fat 27.5g Carbohydrates 13.2g Protein 800mg Sodium

Mediterranean Veggie Bowl

Preparation Time : 10 minutes

Cooking Time : 20 minutes

Servings : 4

Difficulty Level : Average

Ingredients:

- 2 cups water
- 1 cup of either bulgur wheat #3 or quinoa, rinsed
- 1½ teaspoons salt, divided
- 1-pint (2 cups) cherry tomatoes, cut in half
- 1 large bell pepper, chopped
- 1 large cucumber, chopped
- 1 cup Kalamata olives
- ½ cup freshly squeezed lemon juice
- 1 cup extra-virgin olive oil
- ½ teaspoon freshly ground black pepper

Directions:

Boil the water in a medium pot over medium heat. Add the bulgur (or quinoa) and 1 teaspoon of salt. Cover and cook for 15 to 20 minutes.

To arrange the veggies in your 4 bowls, visually divide each bowl into 5 sections. Place the cooked bulgur in one section. Follow with the tomatoes, bell pepper, cucumbers, and olives.

Scourge together the lemon juice, olive oil, remaining ½ teaspoon salt, and black pepper.

Evenly spoon the dressing over the 4 bowls. Serve immediately or cover and refrigerate for later.

Nutrition (for 100g): 772 Calories 9g Fat 6g Protein 41g Carbohydrates 944mg Sodium

Grilled Veggie and Hummus Wrap

Preparation Time : 15 minutes

Cooking Time : 10 minutes

Servings : 6

Difficulty Level : Average

Ingredients:

- 1 large eggplant
- 1 large onion
- ½ cup extra-virgin olive oil
- 1 teaspoon salt
- 6 lavash wraps or large pita bread
- 1 cup Creamy Traditional Hummus

Directions:

Preheat a grill, large grill pan, or lightly oiled large skillet on medium heat. Slice the eggplant and onion into circles. Grease the vegetables with olive oil and sprinkle with salt.

Cook the vegetables on both sides, about 3 to 4 minutes each side. To make the wrap, lay the lavash or pita flat. Lay about 2 tablespoons of hummus on the wrap.

Evenly divide the vegetables among the wraps, layering them along one side of the wrap. Gently fold over the side of the wrap with the vegetables, tucking them in and making a tight wrap.

Lay the wrap seam side-down and cut in half or thirds.

You can also wrap each sandwich with plastic wrap to help it hold its shape and eat it later.

Nutrition (for 100g): 362 Calories 10g Fat 28g Carbohydrates 15g Protein 736mg Sodium

Spanish Green Beans

Preparation Time : 10 minutes
Cooking Time : 20 minutes
Servings : 4
Difficulty Level : Easy

Ingredients:

- ¼ cup extra-virgin olive oil
- 1 large onion, chopped
- 4 cloves garlic, finely chopped
- 1-pound green beans, fresh or frozen, trimmed
- 1½ teaspoons salt, divided
- 1 (15-ounce) can diced tomatoes
- ½ teaspoon freshly ground black pepper

Directions:

Warm up the olive oil, onion, and garlic; cook for 1 minute. Cut the green beans into 2-inch pieces. Add the green beans and 1 teaspoon of salt to the pot and toss everything together; cook for 3 minutes. Add the diced tomatoes, remaining ½ teaspoon of salt, and black pepper to the pot; continue to cook for another 12 minutes, stirring occasionally. Serve warm.

Nutrition (for 100g): 200 Calories 12g Fat 18g Carbohydrates 4g Protein 639mg Sodium

Rustic Cauliflower and Carrot Hash

Preparation Time : 10 minutes

Cooking Time : 10 minutes

Servings : 4

Difficulty Level : Easy

Ingredients:

- 3 tablespoons extra-virgin olive oil
- 1 large onion, chopped
- 1 tablespoon garlic, minced
- 2 cups carrots, diced
- 4 cups cauliflower pieces, washed
- 1 teaspoon salt
- ½ teaspoon ground cumin

Directions:

Cook the olive oil, onion, garlic, and carrots for 3 minutes. Cut the cauliflower into 1-inch or bite-size pieces. Add the cauliflower, salt, and cumin to the skillet and toss to combine with the carrots and onions.

Cover and cook for 3 minutes. Toss in the vegetables and continue cooking for an additional 3 to 4 minutes. Serve warm.

Nutrition (for 100g): 159 Calories 17g Fat 15g Carbohydrates 3g Protein 569mg Sodium

Roasted Cauliflower and Tomatoes

Preparation Time : 5 minutes

Cooking Time : 25 minutes

Servings : 4

Difficulty Level : Average

Ingredients:

- 4 cups cauliflower, cut into 1-inch pieces
- 6 tablespoons extra-virgin olive oil, divided
- 1 teaspoon salt, divided
- 4 cups cherry tomatoes
- ½ teaspoon freshly ground black pepper
- ½ cup grated Parmesan cheese

Directions:

Preheat the oven to 425°F. Add the cauliflower, 3 tablespoons of olive oil, and ½ teaspoon of salt to a large bowl and toss to coat evenly. Lay onto a baking sheet in an even layer.

In another large bowl, add the tomatoes, remaining 3 tablespoons of olive oil, and ½ teaspoon of salt, and toss to coat evenly. Pour onto a different baking sheet. Put the sheet of cauliflower and the sheet of tomatoes in the oven to roast for 17 to 20 minutes until the cauliflower is lightly browned and tomatoes are plump.

Using a spatula, spoon the cauliflower into a serving dish, and top with tomatoes, black pepper, and Parmesan cheese. Serve warm.

Nutrition (for 100g): 294 Calories 14g Fat 13g Carbohydrates 9g Protein 493mg Sodium

Roasted Acorn Squash

Preparation Time : 10 minutes

Cooking Time : 35 minutes

Servings : 6

Difficulty Level : Average

Ingredients:

- 2 acorn squash, medium to large
- 2 tablespoons extra-virgin olive oil
- 1 teaspoon salt, plus more for seasoning
- 5 tablespoons unsalted butter
- ¼ cup chopped sage leaves
- 2 tablespoons fresh thyme leaves
- ½ teaspoon freshly ground black pepper

Directions:

Preheat the oven to 400°F. Cut the acorn squash in half lengthwise. Scrape out the seeds and cut it horizontally into ¾-inch-thick slices. In a large bowl, drizzle the squash with the olive oil, sprinkle with salt, and toss together to coat.

Lay the acorn squash flat on a baking sheet. Situate in the baking sheet in the oven and bake the squash for 20 minutes. Flip squash over with a spatula and bake for another 15 minutes.

Soften the butter in a medium saucepan over medium heat. Add the sage and thyme to the melted butter and let them cook for 30 seconds. Transfer the cooked squash slices to a plate. Spoon the butter/herb mixture over the squash. Season with salt and black pepper. Serve warm.

Nutrition (for 100g): 188 Calories 13g Fat 16g Carbohydrates 1g Protein 836mg Sodium

Sautéed Garlic Spinach

Preparation Time: 5 minutes
Cooking Time: 10 minutes
Servings: 4
Difficulty Level: Easy

Ingredients:

- ¼ cup extra-virgin olive oil
- 1 large onion, thinly sliced
- 3 cloves garlic, minced
- 6 (1-pound) bags of baby spinach, washed
- ½ teaspoon salt
- 1 lemon, cut into wedges

Directions:

Cook the olive oil, onion, and garlic in a large skillet for 2 minutes over medium heat. Add one bag of spinach and ½ teaspoon of salt. Cover the skillet and let the spinach wilt for 30 seconds. Repeat (omitting the salt), adding 1 bag of spinach at a time.

When all the spinach has been added in, remove the cover and cook for 3 minutes, letting some of the moisture evaporate. Serve warm with lemon zest over the top.

Nutrition (for 100g): 301 Calories 12g Fat 29g Carbohydrates 17g Protein 639mg Sodium

Garlicky Sautéed Zucchini with Mint

Preparation Time : 5 minutes

Cooking Time : 10 minutes

Servings : 4

Difficulty Level : Easy

Ingredients:

- 3 large green zucchinis
- 3 tablespoons extra-virgin olive oil
- 1 large onion, chopped
- 3 cloves garlic, minced
- 1 teaspoon salt
- 1 teaspoon dried mint

Directions:

Cut the zucchini into ½-inch cubes. Cook the olive oil, onions, and garlic for 3 minutes, stirring constantly.

Add the zucchini and salt to the skillet and toss to combine with the onions and garlic, cooking for 5 minutes. Add the mint to the skillet, tossing to combine. Cook for another 2 minutes. Serve warm.

Nutrition (for 100g): 147 Calories 16g Fat 12g Carbohydrates 4g Protein 723mg Sodium

Stewed Okra

Preparation Time : 55 minutes

Cooking Time : 25 minutes

Servings : 4

Difficulty Level : Easy

Ingredients:

- ¼ cup extra-virgin olive oil
- 1 large onion, chopped
- 4 cloves garlic, finely chopped
- 1 teaspoon salt
- 1 pound fresh or frozen okra, cleaned
- 1 (15-ounce) can plain tomato sauce
- 2 cups water
- ½ cup fresh cilantro, finely chopped
- ½ teaspoon freshly ground black pepper

Directions:

Mix and cook the olive oil, onion, garlic, and salt for 1 minute. Stir in the okra and cook for 3 minutes.

Add the tomato sauce, water, cilantro, and black pepper; stir, cover, and let cook for 15 minutes, stirring occasionally. Serve warm.

Nutrition (for 100g): 201 Calories 6g Fat 18g Carbohydrates 4g Protein 693mg Sodium

Sweet Veggie-Stuffed Peppers

Preparation Time : 20 minutes

Cooking Time : 30 minutes

Servings : 6

Difficulty Level : Average

Ingredients:

- 6 large bell peppers, different colors
- 3 tablespoons extra-virgin olive oil
- 1 large onion, chopped
- 3 cloves garlic, minced
- 1 carrot, chopped
- 1 (16-ounce) can garbanzo beans, rinsed and drained
- 3 cups cooked rice
- 1½ teaspoons salt
- ½ teaspoon freshly ground black pepper

Directions:

Preheat the oven to 350°F. Make sure to choose peppers that can stand upright. Cut off the pepper cap and remove the seeds, reserving the cap for later. Stand the peppers in a baking dish.

Warm up the olive oil, onion, garlic, and carrots for 3 minutes. Stir in the garbanzo beans. Cook for another 3 minutes. Pull out from the pan from the heat and spoon the cooked ingredients to a large bowl. Add the rice, salt, and pepper; toss to combine.

Stuff each pepper to the top and then put the pepper caps back on. Tuck the baking dish with aluminum foil and bake for 25 minutes. Pull out the foil and bake for another 5 minutes. Serve warm.

Nutrition (for 100g): 301 Calories 15g Fat 50g Carbohydrates 8g Protein 803mg Sodium

Moussaka Eggplant

Preparation Time : 55 minutes

Cooking Time : 40 minutes

Servings : 6

Difficulty Level : Difficult

Ingredients:

- 2 large eggplants
- 2 teaspoons salt, divided
- Olive oil spray
- ¼ cup extra-virgin olive oil
- 2 large onions, sliced
- 10 cloves garlic, sliced
- 2 (15-ounce) cans diced tomatoes
- 1 (16-ounce) can garbanzo beans, rinsed and drained
- 1 teaspoon dried oregano
- ½ teaspoon freshly ground black pepper

Directions:

Slice the eggplant horizontally into ¼-inch-thick round disks. Sprinkle the eggplant slices with 1 teaspoon of salt and place in a colander for 30 minutes.

Preheat the oven to 450°F. Pat the slices of eggplant dry with a paper towel and spray each side with an olive oil spray or lightly brush each side with olive oil.

Assemble the eggplant in a single layer on a baking sheet. Situate in the oven and bake for 10 minutes. Then, using a spatula, flip the slices over and bake for another 10 minutes.

Sauté the olive oil, onions, garlic, and remaining 1 teaspoon of salt. Cook 5 minutes stirring seldom. Add the tomatoes, garbanzo beans, oregano, and black pepper. Simmer for 12 minutes, stirring irregularly.

Using a deep casserole dish, begin to layer, starting with eggplant, then the sauce. Repeat until all ingredients have been used. Bake in the oven for 20 minutes. Remove from the oven and serve warm.

Nutrition (for 100g): 262 Calories 11g Fat 35g Carbohydrates 8g Protein 723mg Sodium

Vegetable-Stuffed Grape Leaves

Preparation Time : 50 minutes

Cooking Time : 45 minutes

Servings : 8

Difficulty Level : Average

Ingredients:

- 2 cups white rice, rinsed
- 2 large tomatoes, finely diced
- 1 large onion, finely chopped
- 1 green onion, finely chopped
- 1 cup fresh Italian parsley, finely chopped
- 3 cloves garlic, minced
- 2½ teaspoons salt
- ½ teaspoon freshly ground black pepper
- 1 (16-ounce) jar grape leaves
- 1 cup lemon juice
- ½ cup extra-virgin olive oil
- 4 to 6 cups water

Directions:

Combine the rice, tomatoes, onion, green onion, parsley, garlic, salt, and black pepper. Drain and rinse the grape leaves. Prepare a large pot by placing a layer of grape leaves on the bottom. Lay each leaf flat and trim off any stems.

Place 2 tablespoons of the rice mixture at the base of each leaf. Fold over the sides, then roll as tight as possible. Put the rolled grape leaves in the pot, lining up each rolled grape leaf. Continue to layer in the rolled grape leaves.

Gently pour the lemon juice and olive oil over the grape leaves, and add enough water just to cover the grape leaves by 1 inch. Lay a heavy plate that is smaller than the opening of the pot upside down over the grape leaves. Cover the pot and cook the leaves over medium-low heat for 45 minutes. Let stand for 20 minutes before serving. Serve warm or cold.

Nutrition (for 100g): 532 Calories 15g Fat 80g Carbohydrates 12g Protein 904mg Sodium

Grilled Eggplant Rolls

Preparation Time : 30 minutes

Cooking Time : 10 minutes

Servings : 6

Difficulty Level : Average

Ingredients:

- 2 large eggplants
- 1 teaspoon salt
- 4 ounces goat cheese
- 1 cup ricotta
- ¼ cup fresh basil, finely chopped
- ½ teaspoon freshly ground black pepper
- Olive oil spray

Directions:

Cut up the tops of the eggplants and cut the eggplants lengthwise into ¼-inch-thick slices. Sprinkle the slices with the salt and place the eggplant in a colander for 15 to 20 minutes.

Scourge the goat cheese, ricotta, basil, and pepper. Preheat a grill, grill pan, or lightly oiled skillet on medium heat. Pat dry the eggplant slices and lightly spray with olive oil spray. Place the eggplant on the grill, grill pan, or skillet and cook for 3 minutes on each side.

Take out the eggplant from the heat and let cool for 5 minutes. To roll, lay one eggplant slice flat, place a tablespoon of the cheese mixture at the base of the slice, and roll up. Serve immediately or chill until serving.

Nutrition (for 100g): 255 Calories 7g Fat 19g Carbohydrates 15g Protein 793mg Sodium

Crispy Zucchini Fritters

Preparation Time : 15 minutes

Cooking Time : 20 minutes

Servings : 6

Difficulty Level : Easy

Ingredients:

- 2 large green zucchinis
- 2 tablespoons Italian parsley, finely chopped
- 3 cloves garlic, minced
- 1 teaspoon salt
- 1 cup flour
- 1 large egg, beaten
- ½ cup water
- 1 teaspoon baking powder
- 3 cups vegetable or avocado oil

Directions:

Grate the zucchini into a large bowl. Add the parsley, garlic, salt, flour, egg, water, and baking powder to the bowl and stir to combine. In a large pot or fryer over medium heat, heat oil to 365°F.

Drop the fritter batter into the hot oil by spoonful. Turn the fritters over using a slotted spoon and fry until they are golden brown, about 2 to 3 minutes. Strain the fritters from the oil and place on a plate lined with paper towels. Serve warm with Creamy Tzatziki or Creamy Traditional Hummus as a dip.

Nutrition (for 100g): 446 Calories 2g Fat 19g Carbohydrates 5g Protein 812mg Sodium

Cheesy Spinach Pies

Preparation Time : 20 minutes

Cooking Time : 40 minutes

Servings : 8

Difficulty Level : Difficult

Ingredients:

- 2 tablespoons extra-virgin olive oil
- 1 large onion, chopped
- 2 cloves garlic, minced
- 3 (1-pound) bags of baby spinach, washed
- 1 cup feta cheese
- 1 large egg, beaten
- Puff pastry sheets

Directions:

Preheat the oven to 375°F. Warm up the olive oil, onion, and garlic for 3 minutes. Add the spinach to the skillet one bag at a time, letting it wilt in between each bag. Toss using tongs. Cook for 4 minutes. Once the spinach is cooked, scoop out any excess liquid from the pan.

In a large bowl, mix the feta cheese, egg, and cooked spinach. Lay the puff pastry flat on a counter. Cut the pastry into 3-inch squares. Place a tablespoon of the spinach mixture in the center of a puff-pastry square. Crease over one corner of the square to the diagonal corner, forming a triangle. Crimp the edges of the pie by pressing down with the tines of a fork to seal them together. Repeat until all squares are filled.

Situate the pies on a parchment-lined baking sheet and bake for 25 to 30 minutes or until golden brown. Serve warm or at room temperature.

Nutrition (for 100g): 503 Calories 6g Fat 38g Carbohydrates 16g Protein 836mg Sodium

Cucumber Sandwich Bites

Preparation Time : 5 minutes

Cooking Time : 0 minutes

Servings : 12

Difficulty Level : Easy

Ingredients:

- 1 cucumber, sliced
- 8 slices whole wheat bread
- 2 tablespoons cream cheese, soft
- 1 tablespoon chives, chopped
- ¼ cup avocado, peeled, pitted and mashed
- 1 teaspoon mustard
- Salt and black pepper to the taste

Directions:

Spread the mashed avocado on each bread slice, also spread the rest of the ingredients except the cucumber slices.

Divide the cucumber slices on the bread slices, cut each slice in thirds, arrange on a platter and serve as an appetizer.

Nutrition (for 100g): 187 Calories 12.4g Fat 4.5g Carbohydrates 8.2g Protein 736mg Sodium

Yogurt Dip

Preparation Time : 10 minutes

Cooking Time : 0 minutes

Servings : 6

Difficulty Level : Easy

Ingredients:

- 2 cups Greek yogurt
- 2 tablespoons pistachios, toasted and chopped
- A pinch of salt and white pepper
- 2 tablespoons mint, chopped
- 1 tablespoon kalamata olives, pitted and chopped
- ¼ cup zaatar spice
- ¼ cup pomegranate seeds
- 1/3 cup olive oil

Directions:

Mix the yogurt with the pistachios and the rest of the ingredients, whisk well, divide into small cups and serve with pita chips on the side.

Nutrition (for 100g): 294 Calories 18g Fat 2g Carbohydrates 10g Protein 593mg Sodium

Tomato Bruschetta

Preparation Time : 10 minutes

Cooking Time : 10 minutes

Servings : 6

Difficulty Level : Easy

Ingredients:

- 1 baguette, sliced
- 1/3 cup basil, chopped
- 6 tomatoes, cubed
- 2 garlic cloves, minced
- A pinch of salt and black pepper
- 1 teaspoon olive oil
- 1 tablespoon balsamic vinegar
- ½ teaspoon garlic powder
- Cooking spray

Directions:

Situate the baguette slices on a baking sheet lined with parchment paper, grease with cooking spray. Bake for 10 minutes at 400 degrees.

Combine the tomatoes with the basil and the remaining ingredients, toss well and leave aside for 10 minutes. Divide the tomato mix on each baguette slice, arrange them all on a platter and serve.

Nutrition (for 100g): 162 Calories 4g Fat 29g Carbohydrates 4g Protein 736mg Sodium

Olives and Cheese Stuffed Tomatoes

Preparation Time : 10 minutes

Cooking Time : 0 minutes

Servings : 24

Difficulty Level : Easy

Ingredients:

- 24 cherry tomatoes, top cut off and insides scooped out
- 2 tablespoons olive oil
- ¼ teaspoon red pepper flakes
- ½ cup feta cheese, crumbled
- 2 tablespoons black olive paste
- ¼ cup mint, torn

Directions:

In a bowl, mix the olives paste with the rest of the ingredients except the cherry tomatoes and whisk well. Stuff the cherry tomatoes with this mix, arrange them all on a platter and serve as an appetizer.

Nutrition (for 100g): 136 Calories 8.6g Fat 5.6g Carbohydrates 5.1g Protein 648mg Sodium

Pepper Tapenade

Preparation Time : 10 minutes

Cooking Time : 0 minutes

Servings : 4

Difficulty Level : Easy

Ingredients:

- 7 ounces roasted red peppers, chopped
- ½ cup parmesan, grated
- 1/3 cup parsley, chopped
- 14 ounces canned artichokes, drained and chopped
- 3 tablespoons olive oil
- ¼ cup capers, drained
- 1 and ½ tablespoons lemon juice
- 2 garlic cloves, minced

Directions:

In your blender, combine the red peppers with the parmesan and the rest of the ingredients and pulse well. Divide into cups and serve as a snack.

Nutrition (for 100g): 200 Calories 5.6g Fat 12.4g Carbohydrates 4.6g Protein 736mg Sodium

Coriander Falafel

Preparation Time: 10 minutes
Cooking Time: 10 minutes
Servings: 8
Difficulty Level: Easy

Ingredients:

- 1 cup canned garbanzo beans
- 1 bunch parsley leaves
- 1 yellow onion, chopped
- 5 garlic cloves, minced
- 1 teaspoon coriander, ground
- A pinch of salt and black pepper
- ¼ teaspoon cayenne pepper
- ¼ teaspoon baking soda
- ¼ teaspoon cumin powder
- 1 teaspoon lemon juice
- 3 tablespoons tapioca flour
- Olive oil for frying

Directions:

In your food processor, combine the beans with the parsley, onion and the rest the ingredients except the oil and the flour and pulse well. Transfer the mix to a bowl, add the flour, stir well, shape 16 balls out of this mix and flatten them a bit.

Preheat pan over medium-high heat, add the falafels, cook them for 5 minutes on both sides, put in paper towels, drain excess grease, arrange them on a platter and serve as an appetizer.

Nutrition (for 100g): 122 Calories 6.2g Fat 12.3g Carbohydrates 3.1g Protein 699mg Sodium

Red Pepper Hummus

Preparation Time : 10 minutes

Cooking Time : 0 minutes

Servings : 6

Difficulty Level : Easy

Ingredients:

- 6 ounces roasted red peppers, peeled and chopped
- 16 ounces canned chickpeas, drained and rinsed
- ¼ cup Greek yogurt
- 3 tablespoons tahini paste
- Juice of 1 lemon
- 3 garlic cloves, minced
- 1 tablespoon olive oil
- A pinch of salt and black pepper
- 1 tablespoon parsley, chopped

Directions:

In your food processor, combine the red peppers with the rest of the ingredients except the oil and the parsley and pulse well. Add the oil, pulse again, divide into cups, sprinkle the parsley on top and serve as a party spread.

Nutrition (for 100g): 255 Calories 11.4g Fat 17.4g Carbohydrates 6.5g Protein 593mg Sodium

White Bean Dip

Preparation Time: 10 minutes

Cooking Time: 0 minutes

Servings: 4

Difficulty Level: Easy

Ingredients:

- 15 ounces canned white beans, drained and rinsed
- 6 ounces canned artichoke hearts, drained and quartered
- 4 garlic cloves, minced
- 1 tablespoon basil, chopped
- 2 tablespoons olive oil
- Juice of ½ lemon
- Zest of ½ lemon, grated
- Salt and black pepper to the taste

Directions:

In your food processor, combine the beans with the artichokes and the rest of the ingredients except the oil and pulse well. Add the oil gradually, pulse the mix again, divide into cups and serve as a party dip.

Nutrition (for 100g): 27 Calories 11.7g Fat 18.5g Carbohydrates 16.5g Protein 668mg Sodium

Hummus with Ground Lamb

Preparation Time : 10 minutes

Cooking Time : 15 minutes

Servings : 8

Difficulty Level : Easy

Ingredients:

- 10 ounces hummus
- 12 ounces lamb meat, ground
- ½ cup pomegranate seeds
- ¼ cup parsley, chopped
- 1 tablespoon olive oil
- Pita chips for serving

Directions:

Preheat pan over medium-high heat, cook the meat, and brown for 15 minutes stirring often. Spread the hummus on a platter, spread the ground lamb all over, also spread the pomegranate seeds and the parsley and serve with pita chips as a snack.

Nutrition (for 100g): 133 Calories 9.7g Fat 6.4g Carbohydrates 5.4g Protein 659mg Sodium

Eggplant Dip

Preparation Time : 10 minutes

Cooking Time : 40 minutes

Servings : 4

Difficulty Level : Easy

Ingredients:

- 1 eggplant, poked with a fork
- 2 tablespoons tahini paste
- 2 tablespoons lemon juice
- 2 garlic cloves, minced
- 1 tablespoon olive oil
- Salt and black pepper to the taste
- 1 tablespoon parsley, chopped

Directions:

Put the eggplant in a roasting pan, bake at 400 degrees F for 40 minutes, cool down, peel and transfer to your food processor. Blend the rest of the ingredients except the parsley, pulse well, divide into small bowls and serve as an appetizer with the parsley sprinkled on top.

Nutrition (for 100g): 121 Calories 4.3g Fat 1.4g Carbohydrates 4.3g Protein 639mg Sodium

Veggie Fritters

Preparation Time : 10 minutes

Cooking Time : 10 minutes

Servings : 8

Difficulty Level : Easy

Ingredients:

- 2 garlic cloves, minced
- 2 yellow onions, chopped
- 4 scallions, chopped
- 2 carrots, grated
- 2 teaspoons cumin, ground
- ½ teaspoon turmeric powder
- Salt and black pepper to the taste
- ¼ teaspoon coriander, ground
- 2 tablespoons parsley, chopped
- ¼ teaspoon lemon juice
- ½ cup almond flour
- 2 beets, peeled and grated
- 2 eggs, whisked
- ¼ cup tapioca flour
- 3 tablespoons olive oil

Directions:

In a bowl, combine the garlic with the onions, scallions and the rest of the ingredients except the oil, stir well and shape medium fritters out of this mix.

Preheat pan over medium-high heat, place the fritters, cook for 5 minutes on each side, arrange on a platter and serve.

Nutrition (for 100g): 209 Calories 11.2g Fat 4.4g Carbohydrates 4.8g Protein 726mg Sodium

Bulgur Lamb Meatballs

Preparation Time : 10 minutes

Cooking Time : 15 minutes

Servings : 6

Difficulty Level : Easy

Ingredients:

- 1 and ½ cups Greek yogurt
- ½ teaspoon cumin, ground
- 1 cup cucumber, shredded
- ½ teaspoon garlic, minced
- A pinch of salt and black pepper
- 1 cup bulgur
- 2 cups water
- 1-pound lamb, ground
- ¼ cup parsley, chopped
- ¼ cup shallots, chopped
- ½ teaspoon allspice, ground
- ½ teaspoon cinnamon powder
- 1 tablespoon olive oil

Directions:

Mix the bulgur with the water, cover the bowl, leave aside for 10 minutes, drain and transfer to a bowl. Add the meat, the yogurt and the rest of the ingredients except the oil, stir well and shape medium meatballs out of this mix. Preheat pan over medium-high heat, place the meatballs, cook them for 7 minutes on each side, arrange them all on a platter and serve as an appetizer.

Nutrition (for 100g): 300 Calories 9.6g Fat 22.6g Carbohydrates 6.6g Protein 644mg Sodium

Cucumber Bites

Preparation Time : 10 minutes

Cooking Time : 0 minutes

Servings : 12

Difficulty Level : Easy

Ingredients:

- 1 English cucumber, sliced into 32 rounds
- 10 ounces hummus
- 16 cherry tomatoes, halved
- 1 tablespoon parsley, chopped
- 1-ounce feta cheese, crumbled

Directions:

Spread the hummus on each cucumber round, divide the tomato halves on each, sprinkle the cheese and parsley on to and serve as an appetizer.

Nutrition (for 100g): 162 Calories 3.4g Fat 6.4g Carbohydrates 2.4g Protein 702mg Sodium

Stuffed Avocado

Preparation Time : 10 minutes

Cooking Time : 0 minutes

Servings : 2

Difficulty Level : Easy

Ingredients:

- 1 avocado, halved and pitted
- 10 ounces canned tuna, drained
- 2 tablespoons sun-dried tomatoes, chopped
- 1 and ½ tablespoon basil pesto
- 2 tablespoons black olives, pitted and chopped
- Salt and black pepper to the taste
- 2 teaspoons pine nuts, toasted and chopped
- 1 tablespoon basil, chopped

Directions:

Mix the tuna with the sun-dried tomatoes and the rest of the ingredients except the avocado and stir. Stuff the avocado halves with the tuna mix and serve as an appetizer.

Nutrition (for 100g): 233 Calories 9g Fat 11.4g Carbohydrates 5.6g Protein 735mg Sodium

Wrapped Plums

Preparation Time : 5 minutes

Cooking Time : 0 minutes

Servings : 8

Difficulty Level : Easy

Ingredients:

- 2 ounces prosciutto, cut into 16 pieces
- 4 plums, quartered
- 1 tablespoon chives, chopped
- A pinch of red pepper flakes, crushed

Directions:

Wrap each plum quarter in a prosciutto slice, arrange them all on a platter, sprinkle the chives and pepper flakes all over and serve.

Nutrition (for 100g): 30 Calories 1g Fat 4g Carbohydrates 2g Protein 439mg Sodium

Marinated Feta and Artichokes

Preparation Time : 10 minutes, plus 4 hours inactive time
Cooking Time : 10 minutes
Servings : 2
Difficulty Level : Easy

Ingredients:

- 4 ounces traditional Greek feta, cut into ½-inch cubes
- 4 ounces drained artichoke hearts, quartered lengthwise
- 1/3 cup extra-virgin olive oil
- Zest and juice of 1 lemon
- 2 tablespoons roughly chopped fresh rosemary
- 2 tablespoons roughly chopped fresh parsley
- ½ teaspoon black peppercorns

Directions:

In a glass bowl combine the feta and artichoke hearts. Add the olive oil, lemon zest and juice, rosemary, parsley, and peppercorns and toss gently to coat, being sure not to crumble the feta.

Cool for 4 hours, or up to 4 days. Take out of the refrigerator 30 minutes before serving.

Nutrition (for 100g): 235 Calories 23g Fat 1g Carbohydrates 4g Protein 714mg Sodium

Tuna Croquettes

Preparation Time : 40 minutes, plus hours to overnight to chill

Cooking Time : 25 minutes

Servings : 36

Difficulty Level : Difficult

Ingredients:

- 6 tablespoons extra-virgin olive oil, plus 1 to 2 cups
- 5 tablespoons almond flour, plus 1 cup, divided
- 1¼ cups heavy cream
- 1 (4-ounce) can olive oil-packed yellowfin tuna
- 1 tablespoon chopped red onion
- 2 teaspoons minced capers
- ½ teaspoon dried dill
- ¼ teaspoon freshly ground black pepper
- 2 large eggs
- 1 cup panko breadcrumbs (or a gluten-free version)

Directions:

In a large skillet, warm up 6 tablespoons olive oil over medium-low heat. Add 5 tablespoons almond flour and cook, stirring constantly, until a smooth paste forms and the flour browns slightly, 2 to 3 minutes.

Select the heat to medium-high and gradually mix in the heavy cream, whisking constantly until completely smooth and thickened, another 4 to 5 minutes. Remove and add in the tuna, red onion, capers, dill, and pepper.

Transfer the mixture to an 8-inch square baking dish that is well coated with olive oil and set aside at room temperature. Wrap and cool for 4 hours or up to overnight. To form the croquettes, set out three bowls. In one, beat together the eggs. In another, add the remaining almond flour. In the third, add the panko. Line a baking sheet with parchment paper.

Scoop about a tablespoon of cold prepared dough into the flour mixture and roll to coat. Shake off excess and, using your hands, roll into an oval.

Dip the croquette into the beaten egg, then lightly coat in panko. Set on lined baking sheet and repeat with the remaining dough.

In a small saucepan, warm up the remaining 1 to 2 cups of olive oil, over medium-high heat.

Once the oil is heated, fry the croquettes 3 or 4 at a time, depending on the size of your pan, removing with a slotted spoon when golden brown. You will need to adjust the temperature of the oil occasionally to prevent burning. If the croquettes get dark brown very quickly, lower the temperature.

Nutrition (for 100g): 245 Calories 22g Fat 1g Carbohydrates 6g Protein 801mg Sodium

Smoked Salmon Crudités

Preparation Time : 10 minutes

Cooking Time : 15 minutes

Servings : 4

Difficulty Level : Easy

Ingredients:

- 6 ounces smoked wild salmon
- 2 tablespoons Roasted Garlic Aioli
- 1 tablespoon Dijon mustard
- 1 tablespoon chopped scallions, green parts only
- 2 teaspoons chopped capers
- ½ teaspoon dried dill
- 4 endive spears or hearts of romaine
- ½ English cucumber, cut into ¼-inch-thick rounds

Directions:

Roughly cut the smoked salmon and transfer in a small bowl. Add the aioli, Dijon, scallions, capers, and dill and mix well. Top endive spears and cucumber rounds with a spoonful of smoked salmon mixture and enjoy chilled.

Nutrition (for 100g): 92 Calories 5g Fat 1g Carbohydrates 9g Protein 714mg Sodium

Citrus-Marinated Olives

Preparation Time : 4 hours

Cooking Time : 0 minutes

Servings : 2

Difficulty Level : Easy

Ingredients:

- 2 cups mixed green olives with pits
- ¼ cup red wine vinegar
- ¼ cup extra-virgin olive oil
- 4 garlic cloves, finely minced
- Zest and juice of 1 large orange
- 1 teaspoon red pepper flakes
- 2 bay leaves
- ½ teaspoon ground cumin
- ½ teaspoon ground allspice

Directions:

Incorporate the olives, vinegar, oil, garlic, orange zest and juice, red pepper flakes, bay leaves, cumin, and allspice and mix well. Seal and chill for 4 hours or up to a week to allow the olives to marinate, tossing again before serving.

Nutrition (for 100g): 133 Calories 14g Fat 2g Carbohydrates 1g Protein 714mg Sodium

Olive Tapenade with Anchovies

Preparation Time : 1hour and 10 minutes

Cooking Time : 0 minutes

Servings : 2

Difficulty Level : Average

Ingredients:

- 2 cups pitted Kalamata olives or other black olives
- 2 anchovy fillets, chopped
- 2 teaspoons chopped capers
- 1 garlic clove, finely minced
- 1 cooked egg yolk
- 1 teaspoon Dijon mustard
- ¼ cup extra-virgin olive oil
- Seedy Crackers, Versatile Sandwich Round, or vegetables, for serving (optional)

Directions:

Rinse the olives in cold water and drain well. In a food processor, blender, or a large jar (if using an immersion blender) place the drained olives, anchovies, capers, garlic, egg yolk, and Dijon. Process until it forms a thick paste. While running, gradually stream in the olive oil.

Handover to a small bowl, cover, and refrigerate at least 1 hour to let the flavors develop. Serve with Seedy Crackers, atop a Versatile Sandwich Round, or with your favorite crunchy vegetables.

Nutrition (for 100g): 179 Calories 19g Fat 2g Carbohydrates 2g Protein 82mg Sodium

Greek Deviled Eggs

Preparation Time : 45 minutes

Cooking Time : 15 minutes

Servings : 4

Difficulty Level : Easy

Ingredients:

- 4 large hardboiled eggs
- 2 tablespoons Roasted Garlic Aioli
- ½ cup finely crumbled feta cheese
- 8 pitted Kalamata olives, finely chopped
- 2 tablespoons chopped sun-dried tomatoes
- 1 tablespoon minced red onion
- ½ teaspoon dried dill
- ¼ teaspoon freshly ground black pepper

Directions:

Chop the hardboiled eggs in half lengthwise, remove the yolks, and place the yolks in a medium bowl. Reserve the egg white halves and set aside. Smash the yolks well with a fork. Add the aioli, feta, olives, sun-dried tomatoes, onion, dill, and pepper and stir to combine until smooth and creamy.

Spoon the filling into each egg white half and chill for 30 minutes, or up to 24 hours, covered.

Nutrition (for 100g): 147 Calories 11g Fat 6g Carbohydrates 9g Protein 736mg Sodium

Manchego Crackers

Preparation Time : 1hour and 15 minutes

Cooking Time : 15 minutes

Servings : 20

Difficulty Level : Difficult

Ingredients:

- 4 tablespoons butter, at room temperature
- 1 cup finely shredded Manchego cheese
- 1 cup almond flour
- 1 teaspoon salt, divided
- ¼ teaspoon freshly ground black pepper
- 1 large egg

Directions:

Using an electric mixer, scourge together the butter and shredded cheese until well combined and smooth. Incorporate the almond flour with ½ teaspoon salt and pepper. Gradually put the almond flour mixture to the cheese, mixing constantly until the dough just comes together to form a ball.

Situate a piece of parchment or plastic wrap and roll into a cylinder log about 1½ inches thick. Seal tightly then freeze for at least 1 hour. Preheat the oven to 350°F. Put parchment paper or silicone baking mats into 2 baking sheets.

To make the egg wash, scourge together the egg and remaining ½ teaspoon salt. Slice the refrigerated dough into small rounds, about ¼ inch thick, and place on the lined baking sheets.

Egg wash the tops of the crackers and bake until the crackers are golden and crispy. Situate on a wire rack to cool.

Serve warm or, once fully cooled, store in an airtight container in the refrigerator for up to 1 week.

Nutrition (for 100g): 243 Calories 23g Fat 1g Carbohydrates 8g Protein 804mg Sodium

Burrata Caprese Stack

Preparation Time : 5 minutes

Cooking Time : 0 minutes

Servings : 4

Difficulty Level : Easy

Ingredients:

- 1 large organic tomato, preferably heirloom
- ½ teaspoon salt
- ¼ teaspoon freshly ground black pepper
- 1 (4-ounce) ball burrata cheese
- 8 fresh basil leaves, thinly sliced
- 2 tablespoons extra-virgin olive oil
- 1 tablespoon red wine or balsamic vinegar

Directions:

Slice the tomato into 4 thick slices, removing any tough center core and sprinkle with salt and pepper. Place the tomatoes, seasoned-side up, on a plate. On a separate rimmed plate, slice the burrata into 4 thick slices and place one slice on top of each tomato slice. Top each with one-quarter of the basil and pour any reserved burrata cream from the rimmed plate over top.

Dash with olive oil and vinegar and serve with a fork and knife.

Nutrition (for 100g): 153 Calories 13g Fat 1g Carbohydrates 7g Protein 633mg Sodium

Zucchini-Ricotta Fritters with Lemon-Garlic Aioli

Preparation Time : 10 minutes, plus 20 minutes rest time

Cooking Time : 25 minutes

Servings : 4

Difficulty Level : Difficult

Ingredients:

- 1 large or 2 small/medium zucchini
- 1 teaspoon salt, divided
- ½ cup whole-milk ricotta cheese
- 2 scallions
- 1 large egg
- 2 garlic cloves, finely minced
- 2 tablespoons chopped fresh mint (optional)
- 2 teaspoons grated lemon zest
- ¼ teaspoon freshly ground black pepper
- ½ cup almond flour
- 1 teaspoon baking powder
- 8 tablespoons extra-virgin olive oil
- 8 tablespoons Roasted Garlic Aioli or avocado oil mayonnaise

Directions:

Situate the shredded zucchini in a colander or on several layers of paper towels. Sprinkle with ½ teaspoon salt and let sit for 10 minutes. Using another layer of paper towel press down on the zucchini to release any excess moisture and pat dry. Incorporate the drained zucchini, ricotta, scallions, egg, garlic, mint (if using), lemon zest, remaining ½ teaspoon salt, and pepper.

Scourge together the almond flour and baking powder. Fold in the flour mixture into the zucchini mixture and let rest for 10 minutes. In a large skillet, working in four batches, fry the fritters. For each batch of four, heat 2 tablespoons olive oil over medium-high heat. Add 1 heaping tablespoon of zucchini batter per fritter, pressing down with the back of a spoon to form 2- to 3-inch fritters. Cover and let fry 2 minutes before flipping. Fry another 2 to 3 minutes, covered, or until crispy and golden and cooked through. You may need to reduce heat to medium to prevent burning. Remove from the pan and keep warm.

Repeat for the remaining three batches, using 2 tablespoons of the olive oil for each batch. Serve fritters warm with aioli.

Nutrition (for 100g): 448 Calories 42g Fat 2g Carbohydrates 8g Protein 744mg Sodium

Salmon-Stuffed Cucumbers

Preparation Time : 10 minutes

Cooking Time : 0 minutes

Servings : 4

Difficulty Level : Easy

Ingredients:

- 2 large cucumbers, peeled
- 1 (4-ounce) can red salmon
- 1 medium very ripe avocado
- 1 tablespoon extra-virgin olive oil
- Zest and juice of 1 lime
- 3 tablespoons chopped fresh cilantro
- ½ teaspoon salt
- ¼ teaspoon freshly ground black pepper

Directions:

Slice the cucumber into 1-inch-thick segments and using a spoon, scrape seeds out of center of each segment and stand up on a plate. In a medium bowl, mix the salmon, avocado, olive oil, lime zest and juice, cilantro, salt, and pepper and mix until creamy.

Scoop the salmon mixture into the center of each cucumber segment and serve chilled.

Nutrition (for 100g): 159 Calories 11g Fat 3g Carbohydrates 9g Protein 739mg Sodium

Goat Cheese–Mackerel Pâté

Preparation Time : 10 minutes

Cooking Time : 0 minutes

Servings : 4

Difficulty Level : Easy

Ingredients:

- 4 ounces olive oil-packed wild-caught mackerel
- 2 ounces goat cheese
- Zest and juice of 1 lemon
- 2 tablespoons chopped fresh parsley
- 2 tablespoons chopped fresh arugula
- 1 tablespoon extra-virgin olive oil
- 2 teaspoons chopped capers
- 1 to 2 teaspoons fresh horseradish (optional)
- Crackers, cucumber rounds, endive spears, or celery, for serving (optional)

Directions:

In a food processor, blender, or large bowl with immersion blender, combine the mackerel, goat cheese, lemon zest and juice, parsley, arugula, olive oil, capers, and horseradish (if using). Process or blend until smooth and creamy.

Serve with crackers, cucumber rounds, endive spears, or celery. Seal covered in the refrigerator for up to 1 week.

Nutrition (for 100g): 118 Calories 8g Fat 6g Carbohydrates 9g Protein 639mg Sodium

Taste of the Mediterranean Fat Bombs

Preparation Time : 4hours and 15 minutes

Cooking Time : 0 minutes

Servings : 6

Difficulty Level : Average

Ingredients:

- 1 cup crumbled goat cheese
- 4 tablespoons jarred pesto
- 12 pitted Kalamata olives, finely chopped
- ½ cup finely chopped walnuts
- 1 tablespoon chopped fresh rosemary

Directions:

In a medium bowl, scourge the goat cheese, pesto, and olives and mix well using a fork. Freeze for 4 hours to toughen.

With your hands, create the mixture into 6 balls, about ¾-inch diameter. The mixture will be sticky.

In a small bowl, place the walnuts and rosemary and roll the goat cheese balls in the nut mixture to coat. Store the fat bombs in the refrigerator for up to 1 week or in the freezer for up to 1 month.

Nutrition (for 100g): 166 Calories 15g Fat 1g Carbohydrates 5g Protein 736mg Sodium

Avocado Gazpacho

Preparation Time : 15 minutes

Cooking Time : 10 minutes

Servings : 4

Difficulty Level : Easy

Ingredients:

- 2 cups chopped tomatoes
- 2 large ripe avocados, halved and pitted
- 1 large cucumber, peeled and seeded
- 1 medium bell pepper (red, orange or yellow), chopped
- 1 cup plain whole-milk Greek yogurt
- ¼ cup extra-virgin olive oil
- ¼ cup chopped fresh cilantro
- ¼ cup chopped scallions, green part only
- 2 tablespoons red wine vinegar
- Juice of 2 limes or 1 lemon
- ½ to 1 teaspoon salt
- ¼ teaspoon freshly ground black pepper

Directions:

Using an immersion blender, combine the tomatoes, avocados, cucumber, bell pepper, yogurt, olive oil, cilantro, scallions, vinegar, and lime juice. Blend until smooth.

Season and blend to combine the flavors. Serve cold.

Nutrition (for 100g): 392 Calories 32g Fat 9g Carbohydrates 6g Protein 694mg Sodium

Crab Cake Lettuce Cups

Preparation Time : 35 minutes

Cooking Time : 20 minutes

Servings : 4

Difficulty Level : Average

Ingredients:

- 1-pound jumbo lump crab
- 1 large egg
- 6 tablespoons Roasted Garlic Aioli
- 2 tablespoons Dijon mustard
- ½ cup almond flour
- ¼ cup minced red onion
- 2 teaspoons smoked paprika
- 1 teaspoon celery salt
- 1 teaspoon garlic powder
- 1 teaspoon dried dill (optional)
- ½ teaspoon freshly ground black pepper
- ¼ cup extra-virgin olive oil
- 4 large Bibb lettuce leaves, thick spine removed

Directions:

Situate the crabmeat in a large bowl and pick out any visible shells, then break apart the meat with a fork. In a small bowl, scourge together the egg, 2 tablespoons aioli, and Dijon mustard. Add to the crabmeat and blend with a fork. Add the almond flour, red onion, paprika, celery salt, garlic powder, dill (if using), and pepper and combine well. Allow rest at room temperature for 10 to 15 minutes.

Form into 8 small cakes, about 2 inches in diameter. Cook the olive oil over medium-high heat. Fry the cakes until browned, 2 to 3 minutes per side. Wrap, decrease the heat to low, and cook for another 6 to 8 minutes, or until set in the center. Remove from the skillet.

To serve, wrap 2 small crab cakes in each lettuce leaf and top with 1 tablespoon aioli.

Nutrition (for 100g): 344 Calories 24g Fat 2g Carbohydrates 24g Protein 804mg Sodium

Orange-Tarragon Chicken Salad Wrap

Preparation Time : 15 minutes

Cooking Time : 0 minutes

Servings : 4

Difficulty Level : Easy

Ingredients:

- ½ cup plain whole-milk Greek yogurt
- 2 tablespoons Dijon mustard
- 2 tablespoons extra-virgin olive oil
- 2 tablespoons fresh tarragon
- ½ teaspoon salt
- ¼ teaspoon freshly ground black pepper
- 2 cups cooked shredded chicken
- ½ cup slivered almonds
- 4 to 8 large Bibb lettuce leaves, tough stem removed
- 2 small ripe avocados, peeled and thinly sliced
- Zest of 1 clementine, or ½ small orange (about 1 tablespoon)

Directions:

In a medium bowl, mix the yogurt, mustard, olive oil, tarragon, orange zest, salt, and pepper and whisk until creamy. Add the shredded chicken and almonds and stir to coat.

To assemble the wraps, place about ½ cup chicken salad mixture in the center of each lettuce leaf and top with sliced avocados.

Nutrition (for 100g): 440 Calories 32g l Fat 8g Carbohydrates 26g Protein 607mg Sodium

Feta and Quinoa Stuffed Mushrooms

Preparation Time : 5 minutes

Cooking Time : 8 minutes

Servings : 6

Difficulty Level : Average

Ingredients:

- 2 tablespoons finely diced red bell pepper
- 1 garlic clove, minced
- ¼ cup cooked quinoa
- 1/8 teaspoon salt
- ¼ teaspoon dried oregano
- 24 button mushrooms, stemmed
- 2 ounces crumbled feta
- 3 tablespoons whole wheat bread crumbs
- Olive oil cooking spray

Directions:

Preheat the air fryer to 360°F. In a small bowl, mix the bell pepper, garlic, quinoa, salt, and oregano. Spoon the quinoa stuffing into the mushroom caps until just filled. Add a small piece of feta to the top of each mushroom. Sprinkle a pinch bread crumbs over the feta on each mushroom.

Put the basket of the air fryer with olive oil cooking spray, then gently place the mushrooms into the basket, making sure that they don't touch each other.

Lay the basket into the air fryer and bake for 8 minutes. Remove from the air fryer and serve.

Nutrition (for 100g): 97 Calories 4g Fat 11g Carbohydrates 7g Protein 677mg Sodium

Five-Ingredient Falafel with Garlic-Yogurt Sauce

Preparation Time : 5 minutes

Cooking Time : 15 minutes

Servings : 4

Difficulty Level : Difficult

Ingredients:

- For the falafel
- 1 (15-ounce) can chickpeas, drained and rinsed
- ½ cup fresh parsley
- 2 garlic cloves, minced
- ½ tablespoon ground cumin
- 1 tablespoon whole wheat flour
- Salt
- For the garlic-yogurt sauce
- 1 cup nonfat plain Greek yogurt
- 1 garlic clove, minced
- 1 tablespoon chopped fresh dill
- 2 tablespoons lemon juice

Directions:

To make the falafel

Preheat the air fryer to 360°F. Put the chickpeas into a food processor. Pulse until mostly chopped, then add the parsley, garlic, and cumin and pulse for another minutes, until the ingredients turn into a dough.

Add the flour. Pulse a few more times until combined. The dough will have texture, but the chickpeas should be pulsed into small bits. Using clean hands, roll the dough into 8 balls of equal size, then pat the balls down a bit so they are about ½-thick disks.

Put the basket of the air fryer with olive oil cooking spray, then place the falafel patties in the basket in a single layer, making sure they don't touch each other. Fry in the air fryer for 15 minutes.

To make the garlic-yogurt sauce

Mix the yogurt, garlic, dill, and lemon juice. Once the falafel is done cooking and nicely browned on all sides, remove them from the air fryer and season with salt. Serve hot side it dipping sauce.

Nutrition (for 100g): 151 Calories 2g Fat 10g Carbohydrates 12g Protein 698mg Sodium

Lemon Shrimp with Garlic Olive Oil

Preparation Time : 5minutes

Cooking Time : 6 minutes

Servings : 4

Difficulty Level : Average

Ingredients:

- 1-pound medium shrimp, cleaned and deveined
- ¼ cup plus 2 tablespoons olive oil, divided
- Juice of ½ lemon
- 3 garlic cloves, minced and divided
- ½ teaspoon salt
- ¼ teaspoon red pepper flakes
- Lemon wedges, for serving (optional)
- Marinara sauce, for dipping (optional)

Directions:

Preheat the air fryer to 380°F. Toss in the shrimp with 2 tablespoons of the olive oil, lemon juice, 1/3 of minced garlic, salt, and red pepper flakes and coat well.

In a small ramekin, combine the remaining ¼ cup of olive oil and the remaining minced garlic. Tear off a 12-by-12-inch sheet of aluminum foil. Place the shrimp into the center of the foil, then fold the sides up and crimp the edges so that it forms an aluminum foil bowl that is open on top. Place this packet into the air fryer basket.

Roast the shrimp for 4 minutes, then open the air fryer and place the ramekin with oil and garlic in the basket beside the shrimp packet. Cook for 2 more minutes. Transfer the shrimp on a serving plate or platter with the ramekin of garlic olive oil on the side for dipping. You may also serve with lemon wedges and marinara sauce, if desired.

Nutrition (for 100g): 264 Calories 21g Fat 10g Carbohydrates 16g Protein 473mg Sodium

Crispy Green Bean Fries with Lemon-Yogurt Sauce

Preparation Time : 5 minutes
Cooking Time : 5 minutes
Servings : 4
Difficulty Level : Average

Ingredients:

- <u>For the green beans</u>
- 1 egg
- 2 tablespoons water
- 1 tablespoon whole wheat flour
- ¼ teaspoon paprika
- ½ teaspoon garlic powder
- ½ teaspoon salt
- ¼ cup whole wheat bread crumbs
- ½ pound whole green beans
- <u>For the lemon-yogurt sauce</u>
- ½ cup nonfat plain Greek yogurt
- 1 tablespoon lemon juice
- ¼ teaspoon salt
- 1/8 teaspoon cayenne pepper

Direction:

To make the green beans

Preheat the air fryer to 380°F.

In a medium shallow bowl, combine together the egg and water until frothy. In a separate medium shallow bowl, whisk together the flour, paprika, garlic powder, and salt, then mix in the bread crumbs.

Spread the bottom of the air fryer with cooking spray. Dip each green bean into the egg mixture, then into the bread crumb mixture, coating the outside with the crumbs. Situate the green beans in a single layer in the bottom of the air fryer basket.

Fry in the air fryer for 5 minutes, or until the breading is golden brown.

To make the lemon-yogurt sauce

Incorporate the yogurt, lemon juice, salt, and cayenne. Serve the green bean fries alongside the lemon-yogurt sauce as a snack or appetizer.

Nutrition (for 100g): 88 Calories 2g Fat 10g Carbohydrates 7g Protein 697mg Sodium

Homemade Sea Salt Pita Chips

Preparation Time : 2 minutes

Cooking Time : 8 minutes

Servings : 2

Difficulty Level : Easy

Ingredients:

- 2 whole wheat pitas
- 1 tablespoon olive oil
- ½ teaspoon kosher salt

Directions

Preheat the air fryer to 360°F. Cut each pita into 8 wedges. In a medium bowl, mix the pita wedges, olive oil, and salt until the wedges are coated and the olive oil and salt are evenly distributed.

Place the pita wedges into the air fryer basket in an even layer and fry for 6 to 8 minutes.

Season with additional salt, if desired. Serve alone or with a favorite dip.

Nutrition (for 100g): 230 Calories 8g Fat 11g Carbohydrates 6g Protein 810mg Sodium

Baked Spanakopita Dip

Preparation Time : 10 minutes

Cooking Time : 15 minutes

Servings : 2

Difficulty Level : Average

Ingredients:

- Olive oil cooking spray
- 3 tablespoons olive oil, divided
- 2 tablespoons minced white onion
- 2 garlic cloves, minced
- 4 cups fresh spinach
- 4 ounces cream cheese, softened
- 4 ounces feta cheese, divided
- Zest of 1 lemon
- ¼ teaspoon ground nutmeg
- 1 teaspoon dried dill
- ½ teaspoon salt
- Pita chips, carrot sticks, or sliced bread for serving (optional)

Directions:

Preheat the air fryer to 360°F. Coat the inside of a 6-inch ramekin or baking dish with olive oil cooking spray.

In a large skillet over medium heat, heat 1 tablespoon of the olive oil. Add the onion, then cook for 1 minute. Add in the garlic and cook, stirring for 1 minute more.

Lower heat and combine the spinach and water. Cook until the spinach has wilted. Remove the skillet from the heat. In a medium bowl, scourge the cream cheese, 2 ounces of the feta, and the rest of olive oil, lemon zest, nutmeg, dill, and salt. Mix until just combined.

Add the vegetables to the cheese base and stir until combined. Pour the dip mixture into the prepared ramekin and top with the remaining 2 ounces of feta cheese.

Place the dip into the air fryer basket and cook for 10 minutes, or until heated through and bubbling. Serve with pita chips, carrot sticks, or sliced bread.

Nutrition (for 100g): 550 Calories 52g Fat 21g Carbohydrates 14g Protein 723mg Sodium

Roasted Pearl Onion Dip

Preparation Time : 5 minutes

Cooking Time : 12 minutes plus 1 hour to chill

Servings : 4

Difficulty Level : Average

Ingredients:

- 2 cups peeled pearl onions
- 3 garlic cloves
- 3 tablespoons olive oil, divided
- ½ teaspoon salt
- 1 cup nonfat plain Greek yogurt
- 1 tablespoon lemon juice
- ¼ teaspoon black pepper
- 1/8 teaspoon red pepper flakes
- Pita chips, vegetables, or toasted bread for serving (optional)

Directions:

Preheat the air fryer to 360°F. In a large bowl, combine the pearl onions and garlic with 2 tablespoons of the olive oil until the onions are well coated.

Pour the garlic-and-onion mixture into the air fryer basket and roast for 12 minutes. Place the garlic and onions to a food processor. Pulse the vegetables several times, until the onions are minced but still have some chunks.

Toss in the garlic and onions and the remaining 1 tablespoon of olive oil, along with the salt, yogurt, lemon juice, black pepper, and red pepper flakes. Chill for 1 hour before serving with pita chips, vegetables, or toasted bread.

Nutrition (for 100g): 150 Calories 10g Fat 6g Carbohydrates 7g Protein 693mg Sodium

Red Pepper Tapenade

Preparation Time : 5 minutes

Cooking Time : 5 minutes

Servings : 4

Difficulty Level : Average

Ingredients:

- 1 large red bell pepper
- 2 tablespoons plus 1 teaspoon olive oil
- ½ cup Kalamata olives, pitted and roughly chopped
- 1 garlic clove, minced
- ½ teaspoon dried oregano
- 1 tablespoon lemon juice

Directions:

Preheat the air fryer to 380°F. Brush the outside of a whole red pepper with 1 teaspoon olive oil and place it inside the air fryer basket. Roast for 5 minutes. For the meantime, in a medium bowl incorporate the remaining 2 tablespoons of olive oil with the olives, garlic, oregano, and lemon juice.

Remove the red pepper from the air fryer, then gently slice off the stem and remove the seeds. Roughly chop the roasted pepper into small pieces.

Add the red pepper to the olive mixture and stir all together until combined. Serve with pita chips, crackers, or crusty bread.

Nutrition (for 100g): 104 Calories 10g Fat 9g Carbohydrates 1g Protein 644mg Sodium

Greek Potato Skins with Olives and Feta

Preparation Time : 5 minutes

Cooking Time : 45 minutes

Servings : 4

Difficulty Level : Difficult

Ingredients:

- 2 russet potatoes
- 3 tablespoons olive oil
- 1 teaspoon kosher salt, divided
- ¼ teaspoon black pepper
- 2 tablespoons fresh cilantro
- ¼ cup Kalamata olives, diced
- ¼ cup crumbled feta
- Chopped fresh parsley, for garnish (optional)

Directions:

Preheat the air fryer to 380°F. Using a fork, poke 2 to 3 holes in the potatoes, then coat each with about ½ tablespoon olive oil and ½ teaspoon salt.

Situate the potatoes into the air fryer basket and bake for 30 minutes. Remove the potatoes from the air fryer, and slice in half. Scrape out the flesh of the potatoes using a spoon, leaving a ½-inch layer of potato inside the skins, and set the skins aside.

In a medium bowl, combine the scooped potato middles with the remaining 2 tablespoons of olive oil, ½ teaspoon of salt, black pepper, and cilantro. Mix until well combined. Divide the potato filling into the now-empty potato skins, spreading it evenly over them. Top each potato with a tablespoon each of the olives and feta.

Place the loaded potato skins back into the air fryer and bake for 15 minutes. Serve with additional chopped cilantro or parsley and a drizzle of olive oil, if desired.

Nutrition (for 100g): 270 Calories 13g Fat 34g Carbohydrates 5g Protein 672mg Sodium

Artichoke and Olive Pita Flatbread

Preparation Time : 5 minutes

Cooking Time : 10 minutes

Servings : 4

Difficulty Level : Easy

Ingredients:

- 2 whole wheat pitas
- 2 tablespoons olive oil, divided
- 2 garlic cloves, minced
- ¼ teaspoon salt
- ½ cup canned artichoke hearts, sliced
- ¼ cup Kalamata olives
- ¼ cup shredded Parmesan
- ¼ cup crumbled feta
- Chopped fresh parsley, for garnish (optional)

Directions:

Preheat the air fryer to 380°F. Brush each pita with 1 tablespoon olive oil, then sprinkle the minced garlic and salt over the top.

Distribute the artichoke hearts, olives, and cheeses evenly between the two pitas, and place both into the air fryer to bake for 10 minutes. Remove the pitas and cut them into 4 pieces each before serving. Sprinkle parsley over the top, if desired.

Nutrition (for 100g): 243 Calories 15g Fat 10g Carbohydrates 7g Protein 644mg Sodium

Mini Crab Cakes

Preparation Time : 10 minutes

Cooking Time : 10 minutes

Servings : 6

Difficulty Level : Average

Ingredients:

- 8 ounces lump crab meat
- 2 tablespoons diced red bell pepper
- 1 scallion, white parts and green parts, diced
- 1 garlic clove, minced
- 1 tablespoon capers, minced
- 1 tablespoon nonfat plain Greek yogurt
- 1 egg, beaten
- ¼ cup whole wheat bread crumbs
- ¼ teaspoon salt
- 1 tablespoon olive oil
- 1 lemon, cut into wedges

Directions:

Preheat the air fryer to 360°F. In a medium bowl, mix the crab, bell pepper, scallion, garlic, and capers until combined. Add the yogurt and egg. Stir until incorporated. Mix in the bread crumbs and salt.

Portion this mixture into 6 equal parts and pat out into patties. Place the crab cakes inside the air fryer basket on single layer, separately. Grease the tops of each patty with a bit of olive oil. Bake for 10 minutes.

Remove the crab cakes from the air fryer and serve with lemon wedges on the side.

Nutrition (for 100g): 87 Calories 4g Fat 6g Carbohydrates 9g Protein 574mg Sodium

Zucchini Feta Roulades

Preparation Time : 10 minutes

Cooking Time : 10 minutes

Servings : 6

Difficulty Level : Average

Ingredients:

- ½ cup feta
- 1 garlic clove, minced
- 2 tablespoons fresh basil, minced
- 1 tablespoon capers, minced
- 1/8 teaspoon salt
- 1/8 teaspoon red pepper flakes
- 1 tablespoon lemon juice
- 2 medium zucchinis
- 12 toothpicks

Directions:

Preheat the air fryer to 360°F. (If using a grill attachment, make sure it is inside the air fryer during preheating.) In a small bowl, mix the feta, garlic, basil, capers, salt, red pepper flakes, and lemon juice.

Slice the zucchini into 1/8-inch strips lengthwise. (Each zucchini should yield around 6 strips.) Spread 1 tablespoon of the cheese filling onto each slice of zucchini, then roll it up and locked it with a toothpick through the middle.

Place the zucchini roulades into the air fryer basket in a one layer, individually. Bake or grill in the air fryer for 10 minutes. Remove the zucchini roulades from the air fryer and gently remove the toothpicks before serving.

Nutrition (for 100g): 46 Calories 3g Fat 6g Carbohydrates 3g Protein 710mg Sodium

www.ingramcontent.com/pod-product-compliance
Lightning Source LLC
Chambersburg PA
CBHW071821080526
44589CB00012B/874